The Populist's Guide to 2020

A New Right and New Left are Rising

By Krystal Ball and Saagar Enjeti

STRONG ARM PRESS
WASHINGTON D.C.

Cover Design: Jake Nicolella
Book Design by Troy N. Miller
Managing Editor: Troy N. Miller

Printed in the United States of America
First Edition

Published by Strong Arm Press
www.strongarmpress.com
Washington, DC

ISBN-13: 978-1-947492-45-5

Contents

Introduction

"American Carnage." That was how Donald Trump famously described the hollowed-out Heartland in his inaugural speech, adding: "We've made other countries rich while the wealth, strength, and confidence of our country has dissipated over the horizon. One by one, the factories shuttered and left our shores with not even a thought about the millions and millions of American workers that were left behind." Pundits gasped and clutched their pearls. How dare he speak the truth about the destruction wrought in our small towns and small cities and in every working-class community. This devastation was not caused by terrorists or a rival nation or an unforgiving Mother Nature, but by our own elected leaders. Politicians in both parties who for decades prioritized profits, GDP, and the interests of their wealthy donors rather than the promises that they routinely made and then ignored, in those all-important de-industrialized swing states.

This was the part of Trump's pitch, more than any other, that the old party establishment had no interest in dealing with. For Democrats, who had passed NAFTA and pushed for TPP and deregulated the banks and let unions wither on the vine, it was much easier to cry "racism!" or "sexism!" or "Russia!" or "Comey!" than to admit that their policies over decades had led directly to this moment. For Republicans, who had spent decades doing whatever the Chamber of Commerce told them to do, it was easier to fixate on the cultural excesses of Democrats than to admit that their own hollow trickle-down libertarian ideology had been completely repudiated when Trump won the Republican nomination.

If any of that self-reflection occurred, establishment leaders and the elite media and the army of pundits that churn out the predictable content that the infotainment industry relies on may have been forced to adjust the lenses through which they view American politics. They may have had to deal with the actual world and the consequences of their actions. Republicans may have had to question whether another tax cut to the rich was really where they wanted to spend their political capital. Democrats may have had to question whether propping up a homogenous group of milquetoast centrists was really the way to win back power and do something meaningful with it. Everyone may have had to think hard about whether organizing our entire society and value system around the god of consumerism had really created the type of nation where we would want to live and raise kids.

We are the hosts of *Rising* at The Hill TV, a daily political morning show that's honestly stunned us both with its rapid success. Our goal at *Rising* is to challenge conventional wisdom and shift both parties to work in the interest of the working class instead of their current financial masters.

Rising has been a daily experiment in what this kind of self-reflection and challenging of the status quo might yield; an experiment in what a dialogue between the most honest elements of the new populist right and the new populist left might look like. How can we shake off the old thinking of the past 40 years and respond to reality and the needs of the people as they exist today? What new lenses can we develop to understand and evaluate what we see in the news and in our communities every day?

The 2020 Democratic primary has been the perfect vehicle to explore these questions. An historically large field has given us a wealth of tiny daily experiments in American politics. We've gotten to witness the pathetic flailing of corporate establishment candidates like Steve Bullock, Michael Bennet, Kirsten Gillibrand, John Hickenlooper, Cory Booker, and Seth Moulton. These were all candidates with the right resumes and calculated positions and donor ties that were supposed to make them serious contenders and likely would have made them serious contenders in years prior. None ever really even got off the ground. We've gotten to watch media darlings like Kamala Harris and Beto O'Rourke, who the media wish-casted into existence as alleged real contenders, before they collapsed due to the utter emptiness of their message. We've seen Elizabeth Warren stumble as she tried to be all things to all people. We've seen the media and the establishment desperately try and fail to snuff out the candidacies of inconvenient outsiders Tulsi Gabbard and Andrew Yang, who both outlasted many more "traditional" candidates. We've seen the limits and frightening possibilities of billionaires willing to buy the elections, whether it's by funding their own campaigns or through willing vessels like Mayor Pete. We've watched neoliberals (those committed to the economic and cultural status quo) freak out as their chosen candidates flop, flounder, and fail. And, as we believed would ultimately happen from the beginning, as other candidates rocketed up and fell out, the two ideological poles of the party, Joe Biden and Bernie Sanders, edged us towards a colossal struggle of generations and theories of change.

Throughout it all, we've watched with alternating frustration and amusement as the media has struggled to make sense of any of this mess—the one consistent theme is how wrong they are about everything. Early on, CNN's crack political analysts Chris Cillizza and Harry Enten predicted that Kamala and Beto would be the top two contenders in the race. Of Kamala, they wrote: "Her profile—an Indian-American and African-American woman with a law-and-order background—looks tailor made for the 2020 Democratic electorate." It would turn out, however, that voters didn't much care about her identity and actively hated her "law-and-order" background. It was a perfect example of the shallow identity politics framing that has caused so many candidates and pundits to fail in their efforts. That same CNN analysis had Bernie Sanders back in 6th place, of course. These well-paid professional prognosticators wondered whether "time has passed Sanders by."

At the same time, elite media has focused like a laser on issues that nobody cares about. While voters routinely tell pollsters and anyone who will listen that they are concerned about healthcare, the environment, immigration, and education, all they've gotten is hour after hour of in-depth coverage of wild-eyed neo-McCarthyism or Ukrainian national security state bureaucratic wrangling. We would humbly suggest that maybe, just maybe, there were other issues to be covered with greater import. For example, as we write this, the U.S. has edged to the brink of war with Iran. Perhaps we could have spent more energy on preventing another endless war, rather than exhaustively trying to sniff out imagined Russian influence under every rock. This is not to absolve Trump of wrongdoing. Krystal in particular has nothing but contempt for him. But open your eyes. Protesters are burning cities and tossing out governments in every corner of the globe. Have you ever asked yourself why? Or wondered whether *our nation* is part of that global conflagration?

As we write this today, no one knows how the Democratic primary or the 2020 election will turn out. But as we dive into the thick of this thing, certain consistent themes have developed—mistakes and biases of the media, hilarious dissembling by the establishment, clues to what will matter and what won't. We decided that now is a perfect time to pull together some of our best work on these themes; to stitch the learnings and analysis from every day into a more cohesive framework that can hopefully help us all understand and better engage with the incredibly consequential events which are unfolding around us every day.

It's easy to feel like every election may be the most consequential of our lifetimes, but today we are staring down several radically different possible outcomes that are best encapsulated in the candidacies of Trump, Biden, and Bernie. In Saagar's view, Trump is the current expression of right-wing nationalism, of a party committed to preserving American identity through control of its borders and protecting its families. In Krystal's view, Bernie is the representative of a left-wing class-based movement that could answer Trump's right-wing populism with something new, a Democratic Party that actually delivers for the entire multi-racial working class. In both our views, Biden is the representative of the centrist establishment holding fast to this idea that if they just eliminated the coarse language from our discourse, they could all get back to their bipartisan commitment to wars, soft corruption, and steady grinding of the working class in the name of efficiency.

In this book, we have mined our day-to-day analysis of the election, searching for the best clues as to what may happen—frames for understanding it. We went back through every morning monologue and op-ed we've done to find the parts that have turned out to be most useful; that seem to best fit the reality that we exist in today, but that few actually understand. We looked for what the candidates, their mistakes, their language, and their fundraising have to say about what new possibilities or old terrors may be born. Because the truth is, we are already living in a new reality. 2020 will be the year when the contours of that new order come more fully into focus.

We've called this book "The Populist's Guide to 2020" because that's how we both identify—as populists. We both believe in putting the massive working class at the center of politics and advocate for candidates and policies which we believe will help accomplish that goal. Krystal is a Democrat and Saagar is a Republican, but we are both first and foremost pro-working class. But this book is really not just for those who share our politics. It's for anyone who feels that the current paradigms for politics don't make sense anymore and wants to understand what a real working class politics looks like. This book will help make sense of this election in a way that is superior to the failure of the old broken frames that the media still relentlessly tries to apply, often with catastrophic results. It is for anyone who wants to actually understand the political realignment we are living through, and not just feed themselves happy talk and outrages of the day curated specially for each side. Viewing the election through the lenses sketched out here, we weren't surprised by Kamala's fall or Beto's failure to launch or Warren's wine-track candidacy or the fact that the race narrowed to a battle between two very distinct theories of change.

We've organized the book into four themes: Core Rot, Media, Identity, and Theories of Change. Each section includes essays from *Rising* that we think were the most significant, relevant, or impactful, along with new original analysis. Taken together, they elaborate and cohere the ideas we grapple with every day.

In *Core Rot*, we explore the oft-ignored reality of America and the world today. Krystal connects the uprisings happening around the globe to our own chaotic politics and protest movements here in the U.S. She examines the deep failings of the Democratic Party, which has left its leaders with no legitimacy to prosecute a moral case against President Trump, as they grasp for straws with red-scare tactics and impeachment. Saagar looks at the wolf in sheep's clothing that is "woke capital" and rips the band-aid off of the ugly truth about the Obama era. He tackles the devastation of so-called "free trade" and lays bare what it says about our nation that our supposed best-and-brightest are mostly enlisted in the service of destroying the working class and American families. Mayor Pete, we're looking at you!

In *Media*, we turn to the structural issues that have caused our national news and online media to consistently miss the biggest stories of our time, and lose their legitimacy with the American public. Saagar dives deep into the way that corporate and oligarchical control of the media causes these institutions to consistently cover for powerful people, to bash or repress working-class movements and obsessively chase the stories that most titillate their affluent cosmopolitan consumers. Krystal delves into her experience at MSNBC to understand how the supposed liberal network became an enemy of progressives and tool of the status quo, while offering a grand theory of why certain candidates are venerated and others trashed by elite media.

In *Identity*, we tackle head-on one of the most fraught and oft-used weapons in the neoliberal playbook: identity politics. We look at what the candidacies of Andrew Yang and Tulsi Gabbard reveal about which diverse candidates are celebrated and which are smeared or ignored. We tackle the claims made by Kamala that she and other candidates of color failed because of racism. We consider why status-quo politics, plus a diverse identity, is such an appealing combo for a certain type of white liberal, and why they are so stunned when voters prioritize ideology, policy, and cultural connections over identity. If you are looking for the ideas that may get us canceled, look no further!

And finally, in *Theories of Change,* we look forward to what may happen next. What approach to politics will actually bring about the change that people keep desperately voting for, in election after election? Who and what will satisfy that 70 percent of the American public disgusted with both parties and appease the 40 percent ready to just burn it all down? Krystal turns a critical eye towards the establishment pro-corporate left, and Saagar to the libertarian pro-corporate right. Saagar warns the left about fixating too much on woke identity politics and permanently losing the more culturally conservative parts of the country that are essential for any working-class movement. Krystal digs into the differences between Bernie and Warren and why those differences attracted completely different coalitions. She also examines how Bernie's time as Mayor of Burlington in the '80s may provide a roadmap for a populist presidency.

To be clear, Krystal's essays published here represent her views alone and Saagar's essays represent his views alone. Our hope however is that taken together, they provide an outline of the new right and new left that will help define our politics for decades to come.

We are living through chaotic, nerve-wracking, and oc-casionally terrifying times, but we hope you will find this book both hopeful and helpful. Nothing has made us more hopeful than our work together on *Rising*, watching what unfolds, laugh-ing at the absurdities, and joining in our outrage at the often bipartisan rituals of manipulating our fellow citizens and view-ing them with contempt. People are often confused by our poli-tics and how much we end up in agreement. Ultimately, we have largely different policy prescriptions and beliefs. However, we do share a central diagnosis of the rot in this country, of how we got to this place, and a deep skepticism of power. It's amazing how far you can get when you start in the same place with a shared understanding of reality. It's a hell of a lot further than the shallow, fake civility politics that the forces of the status-quo say you must embrace-'Keep quiet and hold still while they rip you to shreds.' We take the opposite view. Speak up. Make people uncomfortable. Don't let the "experts" convince you that *better* isn't possible.

— Krystal & Saagar

I.
CORE ROT

Core Rot

By conventional metrics, everything is going great. GDP growth is at record highs, we have historically low unemployment and a sky-high strong stock market. What's more, we live in an era of bounty in certain respects. We can buy flat screen TVs for bargain basement prices and stream every episode of *Friends* whenever and wherever we want. Steven Pinker of "Enlightenment Now" fame summed up this view perfectly in the LA Times saying, "We're living longer, diseases are being conquered, global poverty is being decimated, more kids are going to school, including girls, rates of crime are down, rates of death in warfare are down. Democracy, despite its setbacks in the last couple of years, is much higher than it was even a decade ago."[1] And in certain ways, he's right. Yet, if you go deeper, other metrics paint quite a different portrait.

In our own nation, we are suffering through the worst addiction crisis in our nation's history. More people die every year from opioid overdoses than from car accidents.[2] More die from overdoses every single year than all the American servicemem-

1 https://www.latimes.com/opinion/op-ed/la-ol-patt-morrison-pinker-human-progress-20180321-htmlstory.html
2 https://www.cnbc.com/2019/01/15/americans-more-likely-to-die-from-opioid-overdose-than-car-accident.html

bers lost in the Vietnam War. But it's not just heroin and fentanyl that are killing us. As we've tracked on *Rising*, life expectancy has declined for three straight years, a stunning and unprecedented backsliding in a nation that prides itself for its progress and for its expectation that the next generation will do better than the previous. We are increasingly drinking ourselves to death. For young people the rate of alcohol related deaths increased by 157% over the last two decades. Suicides have spiked too as many are so miserable and devoid of hope that heartbreakingly, they take their own lives. In the deindustrialized Midwest, Northeast, and especially in Appalachia, these numbers are even more devastating.

These grim statistics reveal a deep rot at the center of our society. We were promised that if we just sent more people out into the workplace, and worked more and more hours, and applied for that next credit card so that we could buy all the cheap consumerist symbols of middle class American success, that we would be happier. The cheap Chinese crap that could be ours at low, low prices was supposed to make us content. Is it any wonder that we load ourselves up with debt in search of the happiness that advertisements assure us is just around the corner with that next purchase? Thus, for policy makers, it was more important to Walmart-ize our towns in search of lower prices than it was to maintain the local community businesses that kept wealth local and helped maintain our town centers. Of course, now we sit and watch as Amazon obliterates the suburbs that had already obliterated our town squares.

At the same time, in search of those topline GDP and stock market numbers that we are told indicate a prosperous society, we passed so-called free trade deals, written by the very corporations that hollowed out our industrial core. As factories and steel mills were moved overseas, towns were left with rotting abandoned husks where the pride of the community used to sit. Men who had watched their fathers and grandfathers earn enough and have enough stability to provide for their families on a single income were left scrambling to survive on minimum wage service jobs at Walmart or Wendy's or taking on informal unstable gig work to piece together a living. Even more devastating than the economic struggle though was the loss of meaning, self-concept and self-worth. Our culture tells men their whole lives that the real measure of a man is the ability to provide and then we stripped them of their ability to do so. Is it any wonder that so many are depressed, addicted, angry?

Women are left more often to raise their kids on their own all while also cobbling together a living in low wage service sector jobs. The health care sector is growing and disproportionately employs women. But these jobs are also often low paying, not to mention emotionally and physically exhausting. Today's women may spend their days caring for the children or elderly parents of others, while struggling to piece together care for their own dependents.

Our leaders and national media seem completely oblivious to all of this. If you look anywhere else in the media or on Capitol Hill, all you'll see is Democrats and Republicans at each other's throats. Fighting on cable news panels, yelling on the floor of the House, launching cruel attacks on Twitter. How could it be then that the two of us, with different backgrounds, beliefs, and political identities, find so much overlap on a daily basis? It's not that either of us are shrinking violets. When we disagree with each other, or our guests, we certainly say so. We both view with contempt civility politics that would value being polite to someone's face over uncomfortable truth-telling. This shallow idea of civility is largely weaponized in service of maintaining the disastrous status quo. But more often than not, there's quite a bit of overlap between what we care about and our foundational values.

The truth is, unlike most of the rest of the media which chooses to fixate on the existential importance of the latest outrage of the day, we try to use the stories of the day to illuminate the multi-decade long bipartisan failures, systemic breakdowns, and utter betrayal of the working class. We don't hesitate to call out anyone and everyone who was complicit in creating our current hollow, amoral system. And what's more, the overwhelming majority of America agrees. You are not alone.

An August 2019 NBC Wall Street Journal poll found that 70 percent of Americans say they feel angry "because our political system seems to only be working for the insiders with money and power, like those on Wall Street or in Washington."[3] A large

---

3   https://www.nbcnews.com/politics/meet-the-press/

number of our fellow citizens go even further. In a study focused on identifying the number of voters with a "need for chaos," political scientists found 40 percent believed that "When it comes to our political and social institutions, I cannot help thinking 'just let them all burn.'"[4] A similar number also believed that "we cannot fix the problems in our social institutions, we need to tear them down and start over." You get that? When it comes to our political and social institutions, nearly half of America just wants to let them all burn.

Our entire economy has become increasingly oriented around the special flowers of Richard Florida's so-called "creative class." These are the lucky, mostly college educated, types to whom the entire low-wage service economy caters. The ones who came mostly from big cities or were identified as "special" in their small towns and put on the college track. They are the Pete Buttigiegs of the world whose privilege and particular type of intellect gained them access to the elite world and all the stamps of elite privilege that come with it. The people who expect their sustainable sushi to be available at 2 am and for whom an entire army of exhausted and underpaid workers has been marshaled.

The media has struggled to understand the rage and backlash at Mayor Pete among his own generation, but to us it makes complete sense. He is the perfect emblem of a society that would gather all its brightest minds and weaponize them against the working class—all in worship to the god of "efficiency." He represents the type of person who would view their time at *McKinsey & Co.* as just manipulating spreadsheets with little awareness or care for the human beings whose lives were represented in those numbers.

As a nation, we've been chasing the metrics of topline economic growth, while forgetting that human beings need meaning, worth, and community. A country with a few prosperous super cities and a vast wasteland of hollowed out towns and small cities is not a success. Is it any wonder that voters <u>are increasingly drawn to anti-establishment candidates </u>who are

deep-boiling-anger-nbc-wsj-poll-finds-pessimistic-america-despite-n1045916
4   https://www.nytimes.com/2019/09/04/opinion/trump-voters-chaos.html

willing to tell the truth about the bipartisan failures that have devastated our country and who seem willing to actually fight for something different, or at the very least to tell all the smug elites to go to hell?

Some of these problems are uniquely American, but a quick look around the globe reveals that the world order as we know it is breaking down everywhere you look, see Haiti, Iraq, Lebanon, Hong Kong, France, the UK, Chile and Brazil. There isn't a region of the world without massive protests erupting predominantly among the working class and often across religious and racial lines. Each nation, of course, has its own individual story and sociopolitical dynamic, but there does seem to be a common thread of backlash against corrupt governments and societies that have funneled resources to the top while the working class struggles. In Lebanon, many were pushed into the streets after the government pushed one step too far with a bus rate increase and a tax on Whatsapp. In Chile, protesters were particularly specific about their goals, carrying signs that read: "Neoliberalism was born in Chile and will die in Chile."

The essays in this chapter all speak to this core rot that has left so many in our own nation and around the world hopeless. Whether it's the NBA's decision to put their desire to sell sneakers in China over free speech and democratic values, or the endemic corruption that has rendered Democrats impotent to call out the Trump administration, or the fierce determination of those who benefit from the status quo in maintaining the status quo. The story of 2020 is in many ways a story of the way voters and politicians are reacting to this core rot. Will they once again vote for a more radical and revolutionary choice who will center the working class? Or will the elite keepers of power manage to hang on for another few years? In many ways, this is the central question of our moment. Ultimately the future is clear. The old order will die. It is dying before our eyes. The only question is how long before a new order is born.

Why the World Burned in 2019

Krystal Ball

One of our most insightful regular guests, Matt Taibbi, made a profound and important point about post-Cold War media coverage in his book *Hate, Inc.* After we lost the unifying ratings generator of the Soviet Union as our great enemy, the media had to find another enemy. The new enemy is one another. Watch FOX News and there is no greater foe than the Democrats who are supposedly destroying the country. Watch MSNBC and CNN and it's, of course, the Republicans who are the true evil. This contempt for those of opposing political views doesn't stop at leadership either, it's extended to everyone who supports the opposing party or their ideology. When your fellow citizens are the threat, is it any wonder that every election feels like an existential threat? Is it any surprise that division and mistrust become the norm?

These daily petty intramural squabbles then take on grand importance in the civilizational struggle that is Team Blue versus Team Red. Nancy Pelosi owned Trump! Team Blue must be winning! Trump called Adam Schiff "Shifty Schiff"! Go Team Red! This type of partisan coverage serves two purposes. First, it's great for short-term ratings as fans of either team become infotainment coverage junkies. Although I would argue that in the long term the lasting damage of this type of homerism vastly outweighs any short-term ratings bumps, capitalism always favors the short-term sugar high.

These shallow surface-level disputes serve another important purpose, which is to distract us from deeper problems that don't fit quite so easily into this Team Red versus Team Blue dynamic. It distracts us from stories that may suggest more structural issues in which all elite institutions from our political parties to the media itself may be complicit. 2019 was a banner year for such stories and for the gap between the relative insignificance of the stories obsessively covered and those which were almost or completely ignored. This monologue, originally delivered in October of 2019—before impeachment—is all about that gap. How in the world did we allow ourselves to spend all year distracted and titillated by a Ukrainian phone call, while the globe erupted in flames and we barely noticed?

October 8, 2019

If the history books are accurate, they may well remember 2019 as the year the world began to burn as massive working-class protests rocked every corner of the globe. In Chile, protests sparked by a bus fare hike triggered a mass movement with huge public support to demand an end to the catastrophic inequality of neoliberalism. In Iraq, the country is disintegrating before our eyes as its inept, kleptocratic government, installed after our fraudulent, endless war, falls apart. In Port-au-Prince, Haiti, anti-government protests left dozens dead and scores injured. Meanwhile, in the United States, we get to hear a constant back-and-forth about 'Treason!' and Ukrainegate.

That's right, while the world melts down right before our very eyes, our news media and political leaders have decided to focus their attention on an improper phone call—a phone call by our President that was meant to hold military aid to Ukraine hostage unless they would investigate Joe Biden's son. But, the investigation was never opened and the aid flowed anyway, so what are we really fighting about over here? The idea that Ukraine and Joe Biden were made to feel uncomfortable? The sacrosanct principle of Ukraine's right to Javelin missiles?

Meanwhile, Hong Kong is burning with riots in the streets. Egypt, whose murdering, torturing dictator we arm and support, is falling apart. We continue to sponsor the worst humanitarian crisis of our time in Yemen. ISIS murders with impunity in refugee camps and remains active in northern Syria where we've just abandoned our Kurdish allies to the brutality of strongman Erdoğan. Iran and Saudi Arabia are at the brink of conflict. The yellow vests in France riot. Tunisia has been rioting for a year. Shall I go on?

In the words of the prophetic Will Bunch in the *Philadelphia Inquirer*, "the autumn of 2019 is fast becoming the most revolutionary season on planet earth since 1989 ...the sparks are pretty much the same everywhere. The people we've tasked with running the world have, for the most part, turned out to be corrupt. Did they really think that citizens wouldn't notice?" Bunch, in my view, made this connection powerfully and courageously.

Philadelphia Inquirer
October 6, 2019
Headline: From Baghdad to Kyiv to Haiti, people everywhere are rising up. The U.S. is a big part of the problem.
By Will Bunch

This is why when I see wall-to-wall coverage of Adam Schiff TV, I want to scream. When I hear Democrats wringing their hands about the 'norms and guardrails of democracy,' I feel like I'm taking crazy pills, and when I hear Joe Biden earnestly insist that Trump is some sort of aberration, I begin to wonder if we deserve what we've gotten.

Open your eyes and look around at the world. Or, if international affairs aren't your thing, look around at our own country, where life expectancy is actually in decline. We are rapidly heading towards a recession, domestic terrorism is on the rise, and pretty much everyone is addicted to some stupefying thing, from drugs to porn to Twitter.

Yet, what our elite institutions have decided to focus our attention on, what really brings us into high dudgeon, causing Democrats to launch an impeachment probe that will further strain the fabric of our society, what makes Rachel Maddow "Must See TV," is exactly what Trump said about Joe Biden on that phone call. The fate of the western world hangs in the balance? What if Trump actually tried to use the presidency for his own political benefit rather than conducting the office in an honorable and transparent fashion? Gasp! I'm sure no one has ever done that before. Perish the thought.

I can't wait to have our national attention and decision-making process paralyzed for four months so that we can impotently slap Trump on the wrist with the constitutional equivalent of a strongly worded letter, especially since we already know that the Senate will not convict. And if you want to indulge in the fantasy of imagining Trump actually being convicted in the Senate and removed from office, ask yourself the question, what then? What kind of leader do we get after Trump is gone, when no one has done anything to address the rot of a system that is rigged for the wealthy and the powerful, and a culture that taught us to worship the false God of cheap crap made in China?

Here's some advice. Order your cans of 30-year water, figure out how to make homebrew antibiotics, and buy a mating pair of Irish wolfhounds because, ladies and gentlemen, winter is coming. Or you could just fritter away your time watching palace intrigue infotainment, glued to an impeachment probe with the most predictable ending ever.

Don't miss tonight's episode of a manufactured drama meant to distract you from the terrifying reality that is unfolding every day—if we just bothered to look.

Don't Let Woke Corporatists Fool You

Saagar Enjeti

One of the core teachings of capitalism is that financial entities do not take any action unless it benefits their bottom line. This teaching is often disregarded by woke identitarians when Fortune 500 companies began to parrot their rhetoric through the delusion that corporations committed to profit can bring about social responsibility on their own.

Multinational corporations realized sometime in the mid 2010s that if they began to parrot and sponsor social justice seminars, that these critical race theorists would in turn not criticize them for shipping U.S. jobs overseas and perpetuating the class divide within our society. In effect, they purchased leftist insurance through their woke capitalism.

The alliance between the woke elements of the mainstream media and accumulated capital in American society is a key development as to exactly how we got to where we are right now. The social-justice-obsessed aristocracy within the media, government, and the establishment Democratic party sold a narrative throughout the Obama years that they were pursuing "progress" while simultaneously letting the billionaire class off the hook for internally gutting the country.

This essay is one of my earliest forays on *Rising* in calling out woke capitalism and followed the release of a familiarly anodyne statement from one of the largest corporate trade groups in America, *Business Roundtable.* Business Roundtable adopted the familiar tactic of neoliberals in the Trump-era by expressing concern for American workers by promoting 'socially responsible' CEOs while quietly continuing business as usual.

August 20, 2019

This month, CEOs of the most powerful companies in the United States issued an extraordinary press release through one of their main mouthpieces, seeking to redefine the meaning of what it means to be a corporation. For the first time in history, big business says they no longer believe that the purpose of a corporation is just to deliver maximum profit for its shareholders but to be "truly committed to meeting the needs of all stakeholders" (emphasis added), meaning that businesses, as *The New York Times* puts it, will "invest in their employees, protect the environment and deal fairly and ethically with their suppliers."

Business Roundtable
August 19, 2019
Headline: Business Roundtable Redefines the Purpose of a Corporation to Promote 'An Economy That Serves All Americans'

Don't believe your lying eyes, it's a trap. What they really mean is something much more disquieting.

The people who signed this document include JP Morgan Chase & Co. CEO Jamie Dimon, the CEO of Bank of America, Amazon CEO Jeff Bezos, the CEO of General Motors, and about 200 more like them. In short, these are the people who got us here— they don't particularly care about American borders or American workers, and most of them would and have struck deals with the Chinese government at the expense of you and your family. This press release represents a far graver and more dangerous threat: woke capitalism.

These CEOs know that things right now are fundamentally flawed and pose a real threat to their existing condition. This 'soul searching' statement is anodyne, useless, and meant to distract while they continue with the same old schemes. They sponsor woke social justice causes so that we don't ask too many questions about their Chinese deals, how they treat their workers, or what impact they're having in our country. Much of the media gives them a pass for this because they too are beneficiaries of their largesse.

Corporate power today rivals, if not exceeds, government power. These are smart people who see President Trump, Elizabeth Warren, and Bernie Sanders as threats. They understand exactly which way the wind is blowing. I wouldn't be surprised to see more statements from them about "ethical trade practices" or "investing in workers" as the 2020 campaign rolls on.

The Hill
January 26, 2019
Headline: Likely 2020 Dem Contenders to face scrutiny over Wall Street ties
By Michael Burke and Sylvan Lane

These CEOs know exactly who will be their best friends in government and that's why they're writing massive checks to the likes of Joe Biden, Pete Buttigieg, and anyone else who they think can subsume and direct the populist wave.

Don't let them fool you. Real populism harnesses the concerns of the average worker to leverage the only instrument more powerful than corporations: the power of the people.

Reckoning With The Legacy Of Barack Obama & Joe Biden

Saagar Enjeti

The elite media's love affair with Barack Obama precludes them from conducting any critical analysis as to why Donald Trump won the White House. They instead have perpetuated a narrative since his election that Russian President Vladimir Putin, former FBI Director James Comey, some random Facebook ads, and sexism against Hillary Clinton are the real reasons that Trump is President.

Former Vice President Joe Biden has internalized this narrative and decided to make it the centerpiece of his campaign. He frequently touts his failed neoliberal economic record on the trail as evidence that he has the competence to hold the highest office in the land, with zero recognition that his role in the last forty years of policymaking is exactly what lead to the conditions where Donald Trump could narrowly best Hillary Clinton.

An honest reckoning with the Obama years is nearly impossible to find given how recently it transpired, and there is little political utility in extrapolating a convenient political narrative from misleading surface level analysis. This essay is an attempt on my part to briefly showcase the sorry state of the U.S. economy under the Obama-Biden presidency and the folly of any candidate trying to win the American presidency without acknowledging the failure of neoliberalism over the last 40 years.

November 1, 2019

Former Vice President Joe Biden's campaign is like transporting yourself back into the year 1999. The rhetoric and policy proposals would be the same; the only difference is he says something along the lines of how this election is the "battle for the soul of this nation."

At a November rally in Fort Dodge, Iowa, Biden demonstrated a complete lack of self-awareness and reflection. He remarked on terrible things about American life as if he had no role whatsoever in crafting the policies that lead to these terrible things in the first place. He said that he's "determined to give the middle class a real shot in this country," and that "if we ever lose that, we begin to lose the soul of the country. It's about who we are." I mean, who wants to tell him, folks?

How exactly did the middle class get into trouble? It is absolutely stunning that one of the politicians most responsible for our current plight has the gall to express concern for those he took a direct role in hurting. Biden is, of course, behind the 2005 effort to strip bankruptcy protections for millions of Americans—protections they probably could have used when the bottom fell out of the economy in 2008.

GQ
October 23, 2019
Headline: How Biden Helped Strip Bankruptcy Protection From Millions Just Before a Recession
Biden and Elizabeth Warren have been fighting each other since the 2005 bankruptcy bill.
By Luke Darby

You would think from listening to Biden that he had nothing to do with an administration that oversaw the greatest wiping out of middle-class wealth in generations. You would never know that, in fact, he was a central player. Under the Obama-Biden administration, median household income cratered and then barely recovered to 2007 levels by the end of 2016.

That barely scratches the surface of just how bad things got. In terms of wealth, the median total wealth for Americans in 2016 was 34 percent of what it was in 2007. And when Obama left office, the average wealth of the bottom 40 percent of Americans was negative 8,900 dollars. Throughout all this time, the everyday costs of life went up, which means in a nutshell: you got screwed.

It is difficult to overstate the miserable state that Obama and Biden left this country in. The extremely modest gains made over the course of the Trump administration are a bandaid on the gaping wounds that neoliberals inflicted upon us beginning in the late '90s and 2000s with NAFTA, expansion to permanent normal trade relations with China, and the decision to allow China to enter the World Trade Organization.

Biden's only mention of China during the stump speech was a social-studies-textbook-level platitude answer about how Chinese president Xi Jinping once asked him to define America in a word and he responded, "possibilities." I couldn't help but think that Xi must have turned to his advisors and snickered in Chinese, "yeah, possibilities for us to take advantage of them."

The rest of the speech was filled with all-too-familiar soulless pronouncements about restoring 'dignity' in American politics and restoring our standing in the world. Considering his record, I don't blame voters for feeling that these are empty statements which mean close to nothing. More and more people are waking up to the fact that an Obama-Biden redux would be an abject disaster for our country.

The Real Dangers of a Biden Presidency

Krystal Ball

Few things are more depressing for the future of the Democratic Party, the country, and possibly the world, than the persistence of Joe Biden's frontrunner status in the 2020 primary. Never has anyone been less deserving of frontrunner status. (Okay, perhaps that's an exaggeration, but you know what I mean.) He's inarticulate. He's unimpressive. But that's not nearly the worst of it. The very rot which led to Trump in the United States and other right-wing populist movements around the world was architected in no small part by Joe Biden. And even worse, he still believes in this neo-liberal monstrosity of an agenda!

He still supports the bad trade deals and the deregulation and the hollow civility politics and the wars and the bank bailouts. He has been on the wrong side of nearly every major economic issue of the past 30 years yet has zero self-awareness about it. He'd do it all again and he'll tell you so! In a bizarre way, maybe that is what is actually appealing about him. As I often say on *Rising*, I think he genuinely believes in many of his terrible ideas.

This lack of introspection is also quite convenient, though. It's tough to admit you've been wrong, especially with the many tragic consequences that Biden's decisions have wrought. That's also why he insists beyond all reason that Trump is just an anomaly and, as soon as he's gone, Mitch McConnell and his Senate crew will get right back to working in bipartisan comity with their well-intentioned Democratic colleagues. This delusion keeps Biden from having to admit that he is a major part of the reason that American politics are as screwed up as they are. Just imagine insisting that bipartisan cooperation is imminent when you yourself spent eight years trying and failing to get the Republicans to budge on anything. Biden couldn't even get Republicans to work with him to cut Social Security, something they'd been dying to do for decades!

Let's face it: Biden's general election campaign would be Hillary Clinton 2.0. Trump could easily cast him as another corrupt establishment tool and the result would likely be the same failure Democrats achieved in 2016. For what it's worth, I think he does probably have a better shot than inauthentic wine-track candidates like Pete and Warren, although that's a low bar.

But in many ways, there's a fate that is even more troubling to me than Biden losing to Trump. Let me be clear, I will be voting for the Democratic nominee in all possible imaginable scenarios, but that doesn't keep me from fearing the end result of a Biden presidency. Where will we be after four more years of allowing the rot at the core of America to fester? What cynical and potentially much more ideological and capable demagogue would exploit the opportunity to seize power?

From my perspective, in many ways, the worst thing about Trump isn't what he has done, although there is plenty about his record I find disgusting and horrifying. Ultimately, he's been neutered by his own incompetence, grievance, laziness, and inability to plan for the long term. But he has proven what is possible. He's shown how to pull the levers, and how much latent desire there is for a strong man at the top. He's proven how far people are willing to follow you if you just offer them some modicum of comfort and a sense of power in an often otherwise powerless life.

The following essay is about the very real possibility of Biden as Democratic nominee, and the worst-case scenario that could result from a Biden presidency.

November 19, 2019

As Twitter amuses itself with horrified reactions to Mayor Pete's cringiest, whitest dance of all time, and wealthy donors panic over the fact that not every candidate in the Democratic primary is willing to just parrot their corporatist talking points, a very real and very plausible possibility is being completely overlooked. I know you all don't want to hear this, and I don't really want to say it, but what if Joe Biden actually wins?

Let's think about Biden's campaign so far. Well, let's start with the fact that he mostly doesn't actually campaign, preferring instead to fly to donor events where he says things like "nothing will fundamentally change." When he does show up to face actual voters, he frequently stumbles into either angry confrontations or embarrassing mistakes. He may confidently inform voters that "We choose truth over facts," or that "Poor kids are just as bright as white kids." He may get the state in which he is currently campaigning incorrect. He may snap at any reporter or voter who dares to challenge him.

Then there are his debate performances. Here, for example, is a rather typical Biden answer in response to a moderator question about what Americans can do to repair the legacy of slavery:

Biden: "Well, they have to deal with the — look, there's institutional segregation in this country. From the time I got involved, I started dealing with that. Redlining banks, making sure we are in a position where — look, you talk about education. I propose is we take the very poor schools, triple the amount of money we spend from $15 to $45 billion a year. Give every single teacher a raise to the $60,000 level ...Social workers help parents deal with how to raise their children. It's not that they don't want to help, they don't know what to play the radio, make sure the television — excuse me, make sure you have the record player on at night, the — make sure that kids hear words, a kid coming from a very poor school — a very poor background will hear 4 million words fewer spoken by the time we get there."

Moderator: "Thank you, Mr. Vice President."

Biden: "No, I'm going to go like the rest of them do, twice over. Because here's the deal. The deal is that we've got this a little backwards. By the way, in Venezuela, we should be allowing people to come here from Venezuela. I know Maduro. I've confronted Maduro. You talk about the need to do something in Latin America. I'm the guy that came up with $740 million, to see to it those three countries, in fact, changed their system so people don't have a chance to leave. You're acting like we just discovered this yesterday. Thank you very much."

Ummm...what? Biden has embraced segregationists, fossil fuel executives and Republican talking points. He comes across as loveable and befuddled at best, angrily entitled at worst. He's staked his entire campaign on being BFFs with Obama, yet few in Obamaland have backed him up. Somehow though, through it all, his lock on the top primary spot has barely slipped. In fact, poll after poll shows him still holding steady in that top spot. South Carolina polls continue to show him with a rock-solid hold on the state and overwhelming support among African Americans.

His fellow candidates have basically given up on attacking him. Remember, in the early days, how Cory Booker made a big thing about Biden's embrace of segregationists, even sending the former VP a strongly worded letter? Kamala, who had one of the most memorable debate moments of the cycle with her "that little girl was me" t-shirt-ready-attack-line, which, of course, ultimately backfired on her campaign. These days, everyone's just kind of hanging around waiting for the inevitable, long-awaited implosion of Joe Biden's campaign. But what if it never comes?

After all, immediately following those first four early states where Biden is decently positioned comes Super Tuesday, when sixteen jurisdictions hold their primaries. Included in those primaries are a whole lot of southern states, where Biden is very strong: North Carolina, Tennessee, Arkansas, Virginia, Alabama, and Oklahoma will all go on Super Tuesday. Not to mention Texas, where Biden right now is averaging around a ten-point lead.

On the other hand, actual enthusiasm on the ground for his campaign is literally at zero. At least Mayor Pete's supporters can get energized enough to collectively humiliate themselves with the lamest viral dance of all time. Biden's supporters will theoretically show up to vote for him, but that's it. They don't exist online. At the big Iowa Liberty and Justice event, his sections were essentially boarded up. His 'rallies' are mostly sleepy affairs with just as many curiosity seekers as legit supporters. Have you ever seen a Biden sign, or sticker, or T-shirt? It's really hard to imagine that a campaign with so little visible energy could possibly win, but here we are, imagining it.

Now here's the good news: I do think it is possible that Biden could beat Trump. I don't think he's the strongest candidate by any means, but he's not the worst either. At least he doesn't come off as a condescending elitist who looks down his nose at middle America. When he talks about the grief that has shaped his life, it can be genuinely moving. And at the same time, recent elections in Virginia, Kentucky, and Louisiana have shown that regardless of who the Democratic nominee is, there is a lot of Democratic energy behind beating Trump. I'd be lying if I said he didn't have a shot, even as I believe that Trump will completely own Biden in every debate and that his family's soft corruption allows Trump to just roll out the same playbook he used successfully against HRC.

What really scares me isn't whether or not Biden can beat Trump. It's what he will do if he actually becomes president. Around the world, the globe is melting down in backlash to the neoliberal consensus of which Biden was a key architect and continues to be a firm believer. Look to our own nation, where we've seen wave election after wave election where deep roiling anger rocks the public, and rightfully so. You know the litany of sins: the banking deregulation, bad trade deals, the gutting of everything that makes our communities whole and our futures worth living. Does anyone believe that Joe Biden offers an answer to any of that? Of course not. It's absurd on its face. And what do you think comes next? What do you think comes after four more years of incrementalism and the continued grinding down of the multi-racial working class and continued fattening of the ruling class?

I know it doesn't feel like it, but Democrats got lucky with Trump. They got lucky that he's too short-sighted to take an incremental loss to solidify long term gains. Nothing demonstrates Trump's incompetence as a manager like his deference to Paul Ryan and the staffing of his administration with the same old establishment Republican tools. Liberals lacking imagination believe it couldn't possibly be worse than Trump. They're fooling themselves.

FDR famously wrote during the Great Depression that in order to save the republic it was necessary to be 'fairly radical for a generation.' His New Deal legislation delivered on that vision and helped to build the American middle class. If we offer incrementalism at a moment requiring radicalism, I fear that one day we will long for the Trump era once again.

How Democrats Lost
Their Moral Authority
& Doomed Impeachement

Krystal Ball

Mere days after the commencement of public impeachment hearings in mid-November, I focused on why Democrats would be unlikely to get what they wanted out of the proceedings. It wasn't hard to see in advance what we now know for certain—there was no watershed moment. No bombshell like the Nixon tapes or dramatic crystallizing moment like John Dean's "cancer on the Presidency" moment. The media doesn't have the credibility remaining to make a story land the way Woodward and Bernstein did. As I write this, I understated the case against the Democratic tactics. Because not only were the impeachment hearings in the House a wash, but Trump appears to have strengthened his position for reelection and Independents have moved against impeachment.

Recall that, for years now, cable news anchors and analysts and their paid security state apparatchiks have been predicting the end of Trump, spinning their viewers into a frenzied excitement about how surely the next shoe to drop will be the one. It will be the Russiagate reporting—no, the Mueller report—no, Mueller's testimony—no, the whistleblower complaint—no, the transcript, and on and on and on. How many articles have you read about how "the walls are closing in"? How many predictions about how this next moment would be *the one*? In a sense, with impeachment, the dog has caught the car. And sure enough,

43

Democrats and their media allies have been left with nothing but to claim all they wanted was really some sort of imagined moral high ground and a black mark on Trump's record. As if we hadn't been told all along that they wanted and expected so much more than that.

None of this gives me any joy to say. There's nothing that would encourage me more than to watch Democrats make a competent case against Trump. It's not a hard case to make. He pledged to bring coal back. He hasn't. He pledged to bring manufacturing back. While much of the economy roars, manufacturing appears to have entered a recession. He pledged to deliver on health care and fell on his face. He pledged to be different than your standard Chamber of Commerce Republican and still gave away the store to the rich and the well-connected while throwing symbolic scraps to everyone else. Everyone in the country should know that under Trump, nearly 100 of the Fortune 500 companies paid zero dollars in taxes.

But making this case requires two things that Democrats aren't willing to do: actually grapple with the appeal of Trump and what it says about their failed neoliberal policies, and prove that they would be different. Just imagine if a fraction of the time devoted to Russiagate and Ukrainegate had instead been spent on increasing Social Security, or a $15 minimum wage, or Medicare-for-All. Not only would this time have been spent engaged on issues Americans actually care about, but they might also have actually won some battles too. A certain level of sustained public pressure is impossible for any politician or administration to resist.

Instead, they've chosen to double down on moral indignation of the type that Hillary Clinton tried and failed with in 2016. Most of the analysis of why this approach has failed centers on the idea that "no one cares" and "nothing matters." This is true in a sense and certainly something I've said as well. But there's a danger in this framing as well because it conveniently, once again, lets the powers that be off the hook. It's the public's fault for not caring about what they are *supposed* to care about. In this essay, I offer a deeper explanation. It's not that the public doesn't care so much as that Democrats are themselves deeply compromised and lack the moral legitimacy to effectively make the case.

November 15, 2019

Today, former Ukraine ambassador Marie Yovanovich will testify as part of the public phase of the Democrats' impeachment inquiry. On Wednesday, we heard from State Department official George Kent and Ambassador William Taylor.

Other than our *Rising* live coverage, the most exciting part of Wednesday's hearing came afterwards when Democrats argued online about whether you were allowed to state the very obvious and unavoidable fact that the hearings were boring as hell.

NBC News
November 13, 2019
Headline: Plenty of substance but little drama on first day of impeachment hearings
By Jonathan Allen

NBC's Jonathan Allen, in particular, got dragged for a news analysis piece stating that "the first two witnesses called Wednesday testified to Trump's scheme, but lacked the pizazz necessary to capture public attention." How dare he point out that the Democrats' attempt to create a dramatic Watergate-esque moment collapsed into a ponderous recitation of bureaucratic infighting!

Remember, the whole point of these hearings is supposed to be to change public opinion. Democrats have been explicit that their strategy is to dramatize and bring to life the allegations against President Trump in a way that lands with regular folks. How long have we been hearing that it wasn't really until the impeachment hearings when the public turned on Nixon, dooming his presidency? This was supposed to be the moment when the tables turned, and Republicans buckled under the weight of overwhelming public pressure in favor of removing the President.

The fact that nothing remotely resembling that occurred or is going to occur is not meaningless optics—it actually speaks to the core reason why they are going through all of this. Just consider, *The Washington Post* is currently selling an illustrated graphic novel version of the Mueller report, based on the deeply held belief that if Trump's Russia and Ukraine exploits could just be dumbed down enough for the poor, stupid public, then finally everyone would share in the outrage over Russian Facebook ads and Ukrainian military aid.

Meanwhile, Nancy Pelosi is hailed as a genius resistance hero for her particular technique of "owning" Trump with a standing ovation, launching a doomed-to-fail impeachment probe, and not even batting an eye when he wants to increase the defense budget or provide more funding for border cruelty. Her brilliant strategy will cause leading Democratic candidates to be taken off the campaign trail right at the height of primary season. Of course, Pelosi's unlikely to be heartbroken to see Bernie or Warren sidelined. We all know what she thinks of their politics.

Pelosi's latest attempt to jazz up the interminable inquiry was to accuse the president of 'bribery.' In spite of upping the rhetorical ante, however, even Democrats are conceding that these hearings aren't going to move the public one bit.

CNN Politics
November 14, 2019
Headline: Top Democrats privately concede major shift in public opinion on impeachment unlikely
By Manu Raju and Jeremy Herb

Congressman Jim Himes, a Democrat representing Connecticut's 4th district, explained to CNN that "abuse of power is not necessarily a concept that most Americans run around thinking about. The point is we are all working to try to make a fairly unusual concept to most Americans—abuse of power—understandable."

Actually, Congressman, the American people have zero trouble understanding abuse of power. Why do you think that they've rejected the bipartisan soft corruption consensus so thoroughly? No, what all of this *pizazz analysis* misses is the *real rea-*

son why most Americans are unmoved by Russia-gate and, now, Ukraine-gate. The reason why even voters in the Democratic primary never bring up impeachment or rank it at the top of their priorities. The reason why the candidates who most staked their presidential campaigns on Trump opposition have either exited the race completely or are flailing around somewhere in the low single digits.

It's not because voters are too dumb, or not paying attention, or too racist, or haven't watched enough Rachel Maddow. It's not because Nancy Pelosi hasn't said 'bribery' enough or because State Department official George Kent wore a bow-tie during his testimony.

The reason that no one cares what Democrats have to say about corruption is because Democrats have zero moral authority.

No one buys their outrage or believes that they are impartial actors here. After all, this whole Ukraine-gate issue revolves around a potential investigation into the actual soft-corruption of Democratic frontrunner Joe Biden.

Just this week, Democratic elites pushed Deval Patrick into the presidential race, a guy who parlayed his position at the DOJ helping to settle a massive racial discrimination settlement with Texaco, into a high paying and prestigious job at the company. As Saagar highlighted recently, Congress' Ways and Means Committee Chairman Richard Neal recently presided over a centennial birthday party for AIG, a company that taxpayers bailed out to the tune of $180 billion just a decade ago. Barney Frank, the guy for whom our so-called banking reform bill is named, now sits on the board of a bank!

More broadly, these establishment Democrats are the people who worked in concert with Republicans to ship jobs overseas, deregulate banks, crush unions, and allow corporate monopolies to gain control over nearly every aspect of our lives, only to be rewarded with cushy jobs, gala celebrations, and a permanent ticket into the ruling elite. Americans aren't impressed that Trump's behavior is so radically different than say Hillary Clinton's conduct at the State Department, while her family foundation was sucking up massive overseas cash. They certainly don't trust the Democratic establishment to be the arbiters of moral behavior and good government; not when they still can't even bring themselves to acknowledge that Hunter Biden cashing in on Daddy's name is hardly a noble act.

Allow me to save you the suspense here: the American people understand plenty. It's Democratic leadership that's a little slow on the uptake. Democrats want America to care deeply about these particular presidential norms and guardrails and the rule of law. But when we look around and see that the people who destroyed the economy were never held accountable and in fact are richer than ever; when we see how our elite institutions bent all the rules to protect Harvey Weinstein and Jeffrey Epstein; when we see Hunter Biden on a crack binge whilst making $50,000 per month on a corporate board, it makes all the moralizing about how no one's above the law ring a little hollow. Especially once you remember that young black and brown men are locked in prison for life for the same offense under rules that Hunter's own father created.

I know this argument is likely to fall on deaf ears over at DNC HQ. Perhaps if I put it in graphic novel form, it will be simple enough for the Democratic establishment to finally get it.

Why Democrats Cling to their Russia Obsession

Krystal Ball

The Democratic establishment and their allies in the media have, at this point, thoroughly beclowned themselves with their Russian obsession. Essentially, they took a story that has real merit, Russian manipulation of social media in an effort to sway our election and the clear openness of the current President's campaign in receiving this help, and have turned it into pure insanity.

In order to do so, CNN and MSNBC have brought scores of former spooks and national security state propagandists onto their payrolls who are consistently willing to insinuate that they know more than what they can say publicly, that there is another shoe to drop that will finally lay bare the whole scheme. Thousands of hours of "news coverage" have fixated on Russia paranoia, obsession, and speculation. Jonathan Chait wrote a New York Magazine COVER STORY asking whether Donald Trump was a Russian Asset since 1987. The subtitle was: "A plausible theory of mind-boggling collusion." A plausible theory? Not to be outdone, former naval intelligence operator and current MSNBC analyst and Russia grifter Malcolm Nance offered up his own theory that Trump may have been "under Russian intelligence surveillance for a very long time—as early as 1977."

If you dare dissent from this narrative, you, of course,

will be accused of also doing Russia's bidding, being a useful idiot or perhaps even an "asset." This smearing and crushing of dissent has extended to any critique of the bipartisan neoliberal and neoconservative status quo. Meanwhile, Russia is imagined to be behind virtually every nefarious action in American politics. In these people's addled brains, Russia is somehow behind Tulsi Gabbard's presidential candidacy. Facts be damned. It is taken as an article of faith that she will run third party, splitting off enough of the vote to reelect Trump, even as she has said repeatedly that she will not. This insanity was articulated by none other than former Secretary of State and twice-failed presidential candidate Hillary Clinton.

But Tulsi's candidacy is far from the only place where Red Scare Twitter users (and, yes, even major news organizations) imagine Russian handiwork. As Buzzfeed wrote in a piece titled 'Stop Blaming Russian Bots for Everything,' "Russian bots were blamed for driving attention to the Nunes memo, a Republican-authored document on the Trump-Russia probe. They were blamed for pushing for Roy Moore to win in Alabama's special election. And here they are wading into the gun debate following the Parkland shooting."

The below essay was inspired by a comment I received after I spoke favorably about Andrew Yang's critique of American inequality and the hollow amorality of our meritocratic ideal. According to too many #resistance warriors, Putin must be behind any honesty about the core rot of modern America. Because, of course, the first rule of American rot is that you can never speak about American rot. Doing so may trigger change and, lord knows, we can't have that. Now everyone please get back to your regular scheduled programming. Up next we've got some guy who's willing to say Trump was Russia's puppet since the 1960s! Please fixate on that rather than any of the systemic problems which those of us with power helped to create.

October 11, 2019

Recently, I did a monologue explaining why Andrew Yang made the fifth debate stage while so many others didn't. In my assessment, it is partly due to the fact that he is willing to expose the lie of the American meritocracy. If I do say so myself, it was a very good commentary, so I clipped a portion of it and tweeted it out. Most folks seemed to enjoy it, but at least one viewer had concerns; because this Twitter user replied that Vladimir Putin must have loved my monologue.

Now, I have complicated feelings about this because obviously, a fan's a fan. And if Putin enjoys my work, who am I to say he's wrong? But, it did get me wondering. We've had Glenn Greenwald on this show, and Aaron Maté and Katie Halper and are all set to interview Tulsi Gabbard today, all of whom have been accused by various people on Twitter—and in Tulsi's case, by several so-called 'news organizations'—of being "Russian plants."

Am I *also* a Russian plant? How would I know? Ladies and gentlemen, if you have ever suffered from such doubts, listen closely, because all will be revealed. Here is your comprehensive guide to whether or not you, too, are a Russian plant, at least according to '#Resistance' people on Twitter.

Question one: Have you ever questioned America's endless wars? I don't know if you knew this, but only people who are either paid by Russia directly or are Carter Page-style useful idiots would ever suggest that we end any of our many military engagements around the world. Why? Well, obviously because *Russia* wants us to withdraw from the world. So, if you have ever uttered anything vaguely anti-imperialist, like maybe we shouldn't engage in regime change wars, or perhaps war with Iran isn't the greatest idea right now, or maybe twenty years of war spending to the tune of six trillion dollars and costing hundreds of thousands of lives and destabilizing an entire region wasn't the best decision, then you, according to Twitter, are most definitely Putin's puppet.

Question two. Have you in the past three years questioned the unfailing honor, integrity and sincere intentions of any member of the national security state not named Jim Comey? Did you not pick up on the fact that the architects of torture, mass surveillance, and drone assassination became instantly heroic, just, and always noble in their intentions just as soon as Trump was sworn into office? Well my friend, if you haven't fully made the switch from skepticism to hero-worship of John Brennan, I'm sorry to inform you that you, too, are a Russian plant.

Question three—multiple-choice: Russia-gate was...
a. Watergate times one thousand
b. Watergate times one million
c. Nazism, Pearl Harbor, and Chernobyl, all wrapped up in a traitor pie
d. Incrementally more disturbing than the typical corrupt B.S. that happens in our politics

Question four: Ukraine-gate is...
a. Watergate times one thousand
b. Watergate times one million
c. Nazism, etc.
d. Incrementally more disturbing than the typical B.S.

If you answered "b," Watergate times one million or "c," Nazism, congratulations, you've just been given an MSNBC contract! If you answered "d," incrementally more disturbing than the usual B.S., then I think you already know what you are. I can't believe your Kremlin handlers even let you out today.

Question five. Finally—and this is the one where I really got into trouble with my Yang monologue—have you discussed poverty, addiction, homelessness, the middle class, the working class, gun violence, class warfare, community disintegration, inequality, stagnant wages, consumerism or any of the other ills of late-stage capitalism using facts and data? Well, comrades, let's make some borscht and drink some vodka because there's nothing Putin loves more than Americans telling the truth about the current state of our country.

If I may be serious for a moment. In the 1980s, while the Cold War was still raging, the Soviet propaganda machine was always looking for ways to prove that America was a racist, unequal, violent, terrible place of exploitation and misery. Soviet propagandists made a film featuring Americans living in poverty, with the point being that America was a brutal, terrible place that mistreated workers and left people in squalor. Many of the Americans interviewed in the film were obese, I suppose because the Soviet Politburo types thought that would further highlight

American decadence. Instead, the film had the opposite effect. Ordinary Soviet citizens, who watched the film eagerly to get a rare glimpse of the West, said to themselves...'America is so rich, even the poor people are fat.'

Today, with inequality at the highest level since the Gilded Age, the wealthy paying next to nothing in taxes, children being gunned down in schools, and a massive crisis of addiction, no one needs to use propaganda or lies to make us look bad. Simply telling the truth is a subversive act. And yes, I suppose that I may, in fact, serve Putin or another enemy's short-term interests by doing so. But to look the other way—to hold your tongue—is the most profoundly unpatriotic act I can imagine. Without truth, there is no change. Without change, what are we fighting for? Wouldn't you agree, comrades?

Is Trade or Automation More To Blame For Manufacturing Job Loss?

Saagar Enjeti

The most exciting thing about Andrew Yang's candidacy has been the ability to debate issues of dire national importance. He remains one of the only people in public life, certainly on the American left, who consistently raises the issue of declining life expectancy across the United States, the deindustrialization of the American Midwest, and connecting the loss of manufacturing jobs to the explosion of opioid deaths across the U.S.

Yang's best contribution so far to our national discourse was during a debate between himself and Senator Elizabeth Warren on the matter of whether trade policy or automation is most to blame for the loss of manufacturing jobs in America. Yang claimed to Warren that automation was most responsible for the job losses, which fit his political narrative that a Universal Basic Income is needed to deal with the coming of the fourth industrial revolution.

Warren countered that trade policy is more responsible. In my view, she happens to be correct, and it is important to understand why in order to find out what exactly we should do to return prosperity to American workers. If Yang were correct about automation causing job losses, then we would have seen a rise in productivity after the year 2000 as fewer workers produced more goods. That productivity rise is nonexistent. Instead, we see a drop off in jobs that corresponds with when we established permanent normal trading relations with the People's Republic of China.

On the other hand, Yang may be correct in saying that automation will be more responsible for the decline in future jobs than trade policy. However, acknowledging trade's role in the past is vital for cementing a new and fairer trade policy for the future benefit of the American worker.

This essay was my response to that illuminating moment during the Democratic debate. I make the case that an emphasis on trade policy will secure critical high-tech manufacturing jobs that China currently has its sights set on for economic and national security reasons.

October 17, 2019

A bitter debate has erupted online, and for once it's actually substantive and relevant to all our lives. Presidential candidate Andrew Yang has brought the issue of job loss to the forefront of the 2020 Democratic primary, spurring debate in the entire field of candidates over universal basic income (UBI) versus a federal jobs guarantee. The battle lines were most visible between Warren and Yang during the October 2019 primary debate:

> *Moderator CNN's Erin Burnett: "Senator Warren, you wrote that blaming job loss on automation is, quote, 'a good story, except it's not really true.' So should workers here in Ohio not be worried about losing their jobs to automation?"*

> *Elizabeth Warren: "So the data show that we have had a lot of problems with losing jobs, but the principal reason has been bad trade policy. The principal reason has been a bunch of corporations, giant multinational corporations who've been calling the shots on trade, giant multinational corporations that have no loyalty to America. They have no loyalty to American workers. They have no loyalty to American consumers. They have no loyalty to American communities. They are loyal only to their own bottom line. I have a plan to fix that, and it's accountable capitalism. It says, you want to have one of the giant corporations in America? Then, by golly, 40 percent of your board of*

directors should be elected by your employees. That will make a difference when a corporation decides, gee, we could save a nickel by moving a job to Mexico, when there are people on the board in the boardroom saying, no, do you know what that does to our company, do you know what that does to our community, to what it does to our workers? We also need to make it easier to join a union and give unions more power when they negotiate."

Andrew Yang: "Senator Warren, I just need—I just need to address this."

Burnett: "Go ahead, Mr. Yang."

Yang: "Senator Warren, I've been talking to Americans around the country about automation. And they're smart. They see what's happening around them. Their Main Street stores are closing. They see a self-serve kiosk in every McDonalds, every grocery store, every CVS. Driving a truck is the most common job in 29 states, including this one; 3.5 million truck drivers in this country. And my friends in California are piloting self-driving trucks. What is that going to mean for the 3.5 million truckers or the 7 million Americans who work in truck stops, motels, and diners that rely upon the truckers getting out and having a meal? Saying this is a rules problem is ignoring the reality that Americans see around us every single day."

Burnett: "Senator Warren, respond, please."

Warren: "So I understand that what we're all looking for is how we strengthen America's middle class. And actually, I think the thing closest to the universal basic income is Social Security. It's one of the reasons that I've put forward a plan to extend the solvency of Social Security by decades and add $200 to the payment of every person who receives Social Security right now and every person who receives disability insurance right now. That $200 a month will lift nearly 5 million families out of poverty. And it will sure loosen up the budget for a whole lot more. It also has a provision for your wife, for those who stay home to do caregiving for children or for seniors, and creates an opportunity for them to get credit on their Social Security."

Burnett: "Thank you."

Warren: "So after a lifetime of hard work, people are entitled to retire with dignity."

Burnett: "Thank you, Senator Warren."

For most people, this is a pretty wonky and policy-rich area, understandably causing eyes to glaze over. But determining exactly who is right about this question is actually very important. Per Senator Warren and Bernie Sanders' version of events, American manufacturing jobs were predominantly lost because of bad trade policy pursued by the United States, while according to Yang, trade policy was a small factor but automation was predominantly responsible for the hollowing out of the American middle class.

Yang's case is that since the year 2000, the predominant loss of American manufacturing jobs has been because of automation. This heralds what he and many others have called the 'fourth industrial revolution,' or the arrival of an age where the dominant number of jobs for Americans will be automated out of existence. In order to cope with the dramatic shift in our economy, Yang proposes that a universal basic income of $1,000 a month is necessary to bolster and empower workers.

This is an elegant solution if you believe that this is the correct diagnosis of the problem. This may shock you, but I actually think Elizabeth Warren is right. Bad trade policy is far more responsible for the loss of these four million manufacturing jobs than automation.

If Yang's thesis was correct, then as I said before, we would have seen a spike in productivity after the decline in manufacturing jobs in the year 2000. That, however, has not at all materialized in the data. Instead, Warren and others like myself point to the U.S. beginning permanent normal trading relations (PNTR) with the People's Republic of China. The chart on the following page looks at how jobs fall off a cliff after the signing of NAFTA and the later extension of PNTR with China.

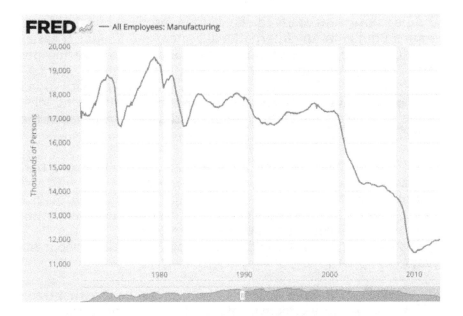

I should give full credit to Yang, as he does have a response to the challenging fact for his narrative that productivity does not spike thanks to all that automation. He believes that productivity remains low because everyone is trying to find a job in order to make ends meet and so they don't leave the labor force. However, Samuel Hammond, Director of Poverty and Welfare Policy at the Niskanen Center, noted on Twitter that:

> *"Declining average productivity growth [does not equal] zero productivity growth. We had higher manufacturing productivity growth in the 1972-2000 period AND steady manufacturing employment levels. If the early 2000s job losses were automation you'd need see (sic) a big spike in productivity."*

I appreciate Yang's passion for this issue because he's right: the rapid hollowing out of our middle class over a period of just 19 years is the central question for policymakers today. This isn't just about job loss; it's about the opioid crisis, it's about suicide, it's about a general malaise and despair at the heart of millions of Americans who feel in their gut that things now are just not right.

The automation diagnosis itself, however, lets neoliberals

Krystal Ball & Saagar Enjeti

and neoconservatives off the hook. They promised us that integrating China into the international system and making it easier for the West to trade with them would allow us to have cheaper goods overall, and to create more jobs here at home. The opposite happened. The discrete policy choice of PNTR with China is overwhelmingly to blame for the loss of manufacturing jobs. China's entire middle class was built at the direct expense of the American middle class.

This is bad news but it's also good news—it means that we have a choice. It means that while automation can, will, and has remained a concern for our manufacturing base, through a radical shift in our trade policy, we can make a choice and bring some of it back. This what candidates like Elizabeth Warren, Bernie Sanders, and yes, Donald Trump have now talked about for years.

While I disagree with Andrew Yang and believe that trade policy is a far more effective solution to this problem than UBI, we would likely not be talking about this at all if it wasn't for his candidacy. It is a great thing to have people online debating how American manufacturing jobs were lost—for a while, nobody even cared, and some were willing to deny the truth. Let's keep the debate going. There's really no downside to trying to do everything we can to reverse the disaster that has been brought upon us.

How To End Our Addiction Crisis

Krystal Ball

One of the most obvious symptoms of the core rot of our nation is the fact that we are suffering through the worst addiction crisis in our history. This problem has become so bad that even the deliberately obtuse media and political establishment has had to pay lip service to it. This addiction crisis is a major part of why life expectancy in America has seen a nearly unprecedented three-year decline. This crisis exposes the hollowness of our topline economic numbers which proclaim to the world: "Look at GDP! Look at unemployment! All is well!"

In fact, all is not well. If all were well, then record-breaking numbers of our citizens would not find the pain of addiction more bearable than the pain of being present in their own lives. Many are familiar with experiments that found that rats placed alone in a cage with the option of regular water and sweetened morphine water would develop a strong addiction to the morphine, eventually dosing themselves to death. What you may not know though is that another set of experiments was also conducted in which rats, which are deeply social creatures, were instead placed in a sort of rat utopia. There were other rats to play and have sex with and a varied environment to explore. The rats were part of a community instead of lonely, estranged, and isolated. These rat park residents had a very different response to the introduction of the morphine water. They preferred the regular water and would only intermittently sample the morphine. They never binged to the point of overdose.

Addiction is a complex disease impacted by social, environmental, and genetic factors. But it's no accident that as an epidemic it would rear its head when so many in our nation have had the rug pulled out from under them in terms of community and meaning. So many of our towns and small cities have been decimated by automation and corporate-driven trade deals. So many of our families have no choice but to send their kids to the same resource-starved public schools knowing that they will never get what they need to ascend to our exalted professional-managerial class. So many of our young men have no hope of providing a stable income backed by middle-class union jobs with solid benefits that their fathers or grandfathers were able to provide. We've sold our lives and our data to Facebook and Google and Netflix, exchanging actual human connection for the sugar high of a fake community.

Our nation's ongoing addiction crisis is one of those areas where Saagar and I align on the analysis of the problem, but diverge on how we should solve it. I believe that the failure of our centuries-long War on Drugs is manifest with deep implications for our own society and for the world. I also believe that our continued doubling-down on the same failed policies is incredibly self-serving. It lets our politicians off the hook from having to think about the deeper structural issues of government/corporate partnership in community devastation, of seeking meaning through consumerism, of putting profit at the center of drug-making. This essay came on the heels of my interviews with Presidential candidates Andrew Yang and Senator Bernie Sanders. I was struck by their very different responses to my questions on the War on Drugs. Here I use those answers to make my case for radical and evidence-based thinking on the War on Drugs and to push Senator Sanders to go further and think harder (to borrow a Yang tagline!) when it comes to decriminalization.

September 19, 2019

Due to a lack of political courage by our so-called leaders, our country is disintegrating before our very eyes. An obvious example of our leaders' failings has been the bipartisan war consensus that has led us to endless regime change wars in both

Iraq and Afghanistan and is now pushing us towards war in Iran. One of the reasons I admire Senator Sanders is that he had the courage and foresight to stand against this consensus even when it was not popular. To this day he stands out for his honesty on the topic.

But there's another endless war that has killed far more Americans and destabilized the world. There's not one region of the world that is unaffected. We have lost 800,000 people in this war in the past thirty years alone. It has cost us more every year than offering free childcare for every family in America would. The war I am talking about, is, of course, the War on Drugs.

In my exclusive interview with Andrew Yang, he became the first candidate in 2020 to take an unequivocal stand in favor of ending this war, telling me that he would decriminalize opiates based on the Portugal model. He said in part: "What's happened is you had people with an OxyContin addiction which has morphed into fentanyl and heroin which are frankly more accessible and sometimes less expensive than the OxyContin that started the addiction chain… I'm for safe injection sites and safe consumption sites. I'm for referring addicts to treatment instead of jail."

That's right. Andrew Yang has committed to ending the pointless and cruel War on Drugs. In our conversation, he told me specifically that he had modeled his policy on Portugal's success. In Portugal, simple possession of any drug, including heroin and cocaine, is not a criminal offense. They don't send people to jail for being addicts, even if the drug they possess is heroin. Instead, they offer treatment, they offer jobs, they offer methadone and other medically based treatment. Portugal's response to catching someone with a 10-day supply of heroin is to offer them help, not prison.

The impact of this change in philosophy has been nearly miraculous. Portugal saw its overdose death rate drop 85 percent since decriminalization. While we lost nearly 70,000 people to opioid overdoses last year alone, Portugal lost only 20 people. To compare apples to apples, since our population is obviously much larger, in Portugal only three people die of overdoses per million. In the US that rate is 185 per million, with numbers even higher regionally. In other words, our century-long experiment with prohibition has utterly and devastatingly failed.

When I sat down recently with Senator Bernie Sanders, I asked a very similar question but received a very different answer. Sanders supports decriminalizing marijuana, but when I asked him about harder drugs he told me: "I'm not there yet." When pressed, Senator Sanders explained that: "Heroin's a killer. You want to push heroin. Sorry, I'm not too tolerant of that." I clarified that we were talking about drug users not dealers, but it didn't change his response.

I understand his hesitation. We have been subjected to so much propaganda about the War on Drugs, that it's hard to accept the truth that prohibition has only pushed people into addiction, putting power into the hands of the worst kind of murderous thugs. Nor do I think that Senator Sanders' position is from a lack of political courage. No man who would advocate allowing currently incarcerated felons to vote is lacking in political courage. Let's just say letting murderers vote isn't exactly a poll-tested position, even though it is, in fact, the right thing to do.

So in the spirit of always pushing our allies to be better, I wanted to lay out a few of the facts of the War on Drugs in hopes that Sanders and others may be inspired by Andrew Yang's courage and knowledge, and evolve to the smart and just position on this issue.

First of all, if you believe that addiction is a public health issue, why are we putting people in jail when they should be receiving treatment? Keep in mind, heroin was invented by none other than good old *Bayer*, purveyors of Bayer Aspirin.

It was actually originally marketed to soothe babies and children nearly 100 years ago, and when it was widely available over the counter, we were not overrun by a nation of zombie heroin addicts. In fact, there were many stable, job holding middle-class people who had a mild, manageable heroin addiction. That is certainly not ideal, but it also wasn't killing more Americans than both World Wars combined. We criminalized alcohol, heroin, and other drugs in this country early in the last century. Somehow while we seemed to recognize that locking people up during alcohol prohibition was a massive failure that only enriched gangsters and led to grotesque violence, we've yet to learn that lesson about other drugs.

In fact, what we did instead was allow Purdue Pharma and the Sackler family to make billions weaponizing a synthetic opioid, OxyContin. But guess what, when your doctor cuts you off of your Oxy prescription after that back injury and you've become addicted, what happens? Many people start buying heroin. Their heroin dealer has no interest in getting them treatment. In fact, the dealer just wants to push the biggest dose. That's why fentanyl has become so prolific.

We drive people into the arms of these merchants of death rather than offering them the help they need. This leads to a downward spiral of increasing addiction and criminality to feed their habit. There are about 500,000 people in this country incarcerated today for non-violent drug offenses, disproportionately, of course, the poor and people of color. Half a million American families have been destroyed. We could have these citizens back and give them the help they need.

But even if you don't care about the moral case for decriminalization, remember: if we decriminalized drugs, the Northern Triangle destruction by drug gangs in Honduras and elsewhere would be curtailed. No drug money, no gangs. Nothing could do more to make those countries livable for their citizens, ending the heartbreaking trail of desperate families seeking refuge here. There'd be no narco-gang dollars to destabilize Mexico. We wouldn't be funding the Taliban through their shipments of opium poppy heroin.

We have been attempting to end drug use through prohibition for more than 100 years, and yet here we are, with the worst addiction crisis in our nation's history. It is time to admit this policy has failed. And while full decriminalization may seem radical, what's truly insane is staying the course. So, Senator Sanders, please, follow the lead of Andrew Yang and bring your voice of courage and moral clarity to end the biggest endless war of them all, the War on Drugs. We must not let another 800,000 people die needlessly out of propaganda, fear, and Big Pharma greed.

A McKinsey Presidency Would Be A Hellish Future

Saagar Enjeti

For a candidate like Mayor Pete, who bills himself as some sort of champion for the middle class, small towns, and the industrial Midwest, he sure does speak highly of his time working at McKinsey and Company—a massive corporate "consulting" racket designed to help businesses maximize profit off the backs of the working class and families. From the group's efforts on the 2008 financial crisis to their influence of Chinese businesses to promote their efforts to expand artificial islands in the South China Sea, it is clear that the company's mission is not necessarily to benefit America.

Just last year, for example, according to *The New York Times*, "the Massachusetts attorney general said McKinsey had helped the maker of OxyContin fan the flames of the opioid epidemic" and that the consultancy firm recommended ideas to Purdue Pharma on how they could "turbocharge sales of OxyContin" in order to "counter efforts by drug enforcement agents to reduce opioid use."

Buttigieg has faced controversy for his willingness to speak highly about the firm, and for his insistence that he keep much of what he did there private. This should worry every single voter. Let me be clear: this world-wide, shady management consulting firm doesn't care about you, your family, or our country. Buttigieg represents that same worldview.

In this essay, I shed some light on the controversy that has surrounded Buttigieg's campaign, and explain why his work at the firm represents something much larger and more destructive than anyone could imagine.

December 12, 2019

Mayor Pete Buttigieg's past work for McKinsey & Co. has caused quite a stir. The most extreme parts of the left say that his very work for the company is disqualifying, while the neoliberal left and the libertarian right are defending the mayor's work as that done by a 25-year-old to simply increase productivity for businesses, which is something we value in our economy, right? In my view, the situation is a lot more complicated.

Buttigieg caved to public pressure in December of 2019 when he released the clients he worked for while at McKinsey, characterizing his work as mostly working on spreadsheets with no managerial responsibility. If you take a look at the circumstances of his employment, it seems that he is probably telling the truth. But the problem isn't necessarily the work that Buttigieg did there, it's his attitude towards the company and the economy at large, especially after that experience.

Buttigieg should be outraged at the lies that were fed to him as a credentialed member of the neoliberal meritocratic elite. This is a kid who clearly wanted to get involved in public service. He went to Harvard where he majored in history and literature, he won a Rhodes scholarship like former president Bill Clinton, and expressed a love for politics with some short stints on presidential campaigns. But within these elite institutions, they indoctrinate students that their "talents" as a young person are best served at places like McKinsey & Co.

So, he went off to that to that company in 2007 to help the likes of Blue Cross Blue Shield in Michigan fire people and to engage in various other soulless compliance gigs. The takeaway from that experience should have been that much of this business is about taking the best and brightest within the United States and putting them to work at extracting as much wealth as they possibly can from the rest of the country. These companies financialize and commoditize, all so that fellow Harvard graduates on Wall Street can gamble with their profits.

As Anand Giridharadas put it in a tweet, "If you've worked at McKinsey in this era, the issue isn't just certain clients. It's that, even at its best, much of the work is about increasing investors' share of profits by reducing labor's share. It's what I've tried to make good on and speak truth on."

But what was Pete Buttigieg's takeaway from that experience? It wasn't that he had been a cog in a soulless machine whose purpose has generally been to recommend offshoring, unbundling, firing, and automating as many members of the working class as possible. Instead, he joined the U.S. military, moved home, and touted his McKinsey record as a reason why he was qualified for the job of trying to reimagine the city budget of South Bend, Indiana.

Current Affairs
March 29, 2019
Headline: All About Pete
Only accept politicians who have proved they actually care about people other than themselves...
By Nathan J. Robinson

As Nathan J. Robinson pointed out over at *Current Affairs*, Pete has written that McKinsey was his most "intellectually forming experience" and that ultimately he only left because it "could not furnish that deep level of purpose that I craved." When he was asked in an early interview about McKinsey's more problematic work for authoritarian regimes, he said:

> "You don't see blanket denunciations of law firms that serve any number of these clients, because the thought is just, client service is what it is. And you serve people and represent their interests. But there seems to be a higher expectation of consultancies."

Buttigieg says he is proud of his past work, and that he is proud of his past company. When he says here that these companies "serve people and represent their interests," he means serving people that can afford million-dollar contracts and the interests of the rich and powerful coastal elites. Therein lies the problem with Buttigieg's entire candidacy: he fundamentally does not believe that the structure of the American economy is bad. He doesn't think that profit engineering at the expense of American workers is something to be mitigated. That's why billionaires and rich older voters love him, because the economy is working just fine for them, and Buttigieg is here to serve and represent their interests.

The Story Behind
The NBA-China Debacle

Saagar Enjeti

No single episode of 2019 better illustrated the current predicament of the U.S. economy than the NBA's capitulation to Chinese interests. The NBA, like all U.S. corporations, became seduced by promises of exploding revenue in the one-billion-person Chinese market and accepted a whole host of authoritarian demands by that government in return for sizeable profits.

This same action played out across dozens of industries from manufacturing to Hollywood and Wall Street. The end result is a robust Chinese state that has absolutely no qualms using its financial entanglements with U.S. corporations to try and push its domestic political agenda right here at home.

U.S. corporations' willingness to sell out American citizens in exchange for Chinese cash mirrors American monopolies' tacit cooperation with the Nazi regime before the outbreak of World War II. Concentrated capital shares no national allegiance and will always work to maximize the bottom line, no matter who suffers.

This essay underscores one of the key failures of the neoliberal consensus that governed the United States in the post-Cold War era. Politicians like Bill Clinton and Joe Biden told us that normalizing trade relations with China would lead to cheaper prices in the U.S., and more democratization in their authoritarian system. Instead what has happened is that the U.S. is now importing Chinese autocracy on top of losing its domestic capacity to manufacture things critical for its sustainability as an independent nation. The market is not capable of protecting the integrity of our nation: only the government can do that.

October 8, 2019

The Chinese government is very upset at Houston Rockets General Manager Daryl Morey for tweeting support for the protesters in Hong Kong—so much so that they're banning video streams of the Rockets and forcing Chinese companies to back out of lucrative advertising and merchandising deals with the team. This is straight out of China's economic warfare playbook, and the real problem is that it appeared to almost work.

The owner of the Houston Rockets quickly distanced himself from Morey's tweet, and the NBA itself put out a statement calling Morey's expression of support for Hong Kong protestors "regrettable," urging reconciliation with its fans in China. Here's the NBA's ridiculous statement:

> *"We recognize that the views expressed by Houston Rockets General Manager Daryl Morey have deeply offended many of our friends and fans in China, which is regrettable. While Daryl has made it clear that his tweet does not represent the Rockets or the NBA, the values of the league support individuals' educating themselves and sharing their views on matters important to them. We have great respect for the history and culture of China and hope that sports and the NBA can be used as a unifying force to bridge cultural divides and bring people together."*

This was a clear bootlicking attempt by the Houston Rockets and the league to beg for Chinese cash, and this perfectly encapsulates the story of how corporations and the billionaire class sold us all out a very long time ago. The magnitude of the problem we face is grave. Take a look at this disgraceful statement by Brooklyn Nets owner Joe Tsai:

> *"I am going into all of this because a student of history will understand that the Chinese psyche has heavy baggage when it*

comes to any threat, foreign or domestic, to carve up Chinese territories. When the topic of any separatist movement comes up, Chinese people feel a strong sense of shame and anger because of this history of foreign occupation. By now I hope you can begin to understand why the Daryl Morey tweet is so damaging to the relationship with our fans in China. I don't know Daryl personally. I am sure he's a fine NBA general manager, and I will take at face value his subsequent apology that he was not as well informed as he should have been. But the hurt that this incident has caused will take a long time to repair. I hope to help the League to move on from this incident. I will continue to be an outspoken NBA Governor on issues that are important to China. I ask that our Chinese fans keep the faith in what the NBA and basketball can do to unite people from all over the world."

It's easier to make sense of this odd capitulation to the Chinese over Western interests when you realize that Tsai, in addition to being an NBA owner, is also the executive chairman of Alibaba Group—one of the largest corporations in China. Even Rockets players got in on the action. Star athlete James Harden apologized for the tweet of his General Manager. Why? Well, a quick Google search tells me that he signed a gigantic endorsement deal with Adidas and has been on tour in China for many years promoting his products.

These people don't give a damn about the United States. They care about making money. The NBA is just the tip of the iceberg. Presidential candidate and billionaire Michael Bloomberg debased himself in a September 2019 PBS Firing Line interview, where he denied that Chinese 'President' Xi Jinping is a dictator: "The Communist Party wants to stay in power in China and they listen to the public...Xi Jinping is not a dictator. He has to satisfy his constituents or he's not going to survive."

Bloomberg isn't a dumb guy. I couldn't believe what he said until a trusted source pointed out that Bloomberg just added Chinese corporate bonds to its index funds. Then it all made sense. Follow the money.

How did we get to a place where our biggest stars and richest among us don't care about us? It's a bipartisan tale that starts in the 1980s when American corporations saw the rise of a relatively stable China following years of turmoil. China promised American corporations a cheaper place to make their products so they didn't have to pay or provide healthcare to those pesky American citizens. These corporations used their power in the White House, in Congress, and in the media to push a central narrative: that opening China up to economic investment from the West would make our two economies intertwined and therefore create a more democratic society.

At the same time, American consumers get cheaper goods from China, so it's a win-win for everybody, right? Wrong. Instead what happened is that the industrial Midwest rapidly deindustrialized. The Chinese middle class, though, grew faster than anyone expected, and a once provincial backwater became America's largest competitor on the global stage. The entire time, while you were suffering from these policies, every think-tank scholar and politician in Washington, on both sides of the aisle, told you over and over again that you were better off because goods were cheaper.

Our populace is literally poisoning itself with drugs, people are killing themselves at historically high rates, wealth inequality is worse than it's ever been. Meanwhile, Wall Street, Hollywood, the NBA, and nearly every other part of the commanding heights of American culture has been infested with Chinese cash.

Why is that a bad thing? Because now the people who control our banks, who control what we see, what we laugh at, who we watch play sports, are all now beholden to some very bad people in Beijing. And Beijing isn't shy about using its economic entanglements with us to try and force American citizens to behave however they'd like, as evidenced by this NBA scandal.

As I said before, the NBA is just the tip of the iceberg. People were puzzled when a new trailer debuted for Top Gun 2, where they saw that the iconic 'Top Gun' leather jacket, originally with Japanese and Taiwanese flag patches, was changed to appease the Chinese movie studio cartel. The producers of the film wanted to have a better chance of breaking into the lucrative Chinese movie market. The film, just one example out of many, is financed by Tencent Pictures, owned by Tencent, a massive Chinese state-controlled media conglomerate.

At no other time in the history of our country, however, has there been such strong financial interests for the richest in our economy to side with our enemies over our own citizens. Corporate leaders don't care about you, but worse—they have constructed an ideology which lets them justify the empowerment of our enemies in the name of 'cheaper' imported products for us all.

II.
MEDIA

Media

Trust in the media has plummeted as citizens realize that elite media institutions are more interested in pandering to their respective political bases for profit than in truly informing the public. How else can you explain the stories they hype exhaustively, the stories they ignore, and the consistent spin and manipulation of facts to fit partisan narratives? Their real unstated agenda though is even more insidious than just partisan cheerleading. Their real agenda is covering and advocating for the interests of the bipartisan cosmopolitan elite.

After all, the affluent, culturally dominant, creative class is their customer base, populates their newsrooms, and surrounds them every day. That's why, to the extent the working class exists at all in most elite media circles, they are caricatured at best, derided at worst. Just consider how many "let's go on a safari in the heartland to try and understand this peculiar species" style packages that we've all been collectively subjected to since Trump's election.

You can take it from us. One of us is a former MSNBC anchor who was essentially silenced by the network for daring to ask former Secretary of State Hillary Clinton not to run for President. The other was a White House correspondent during the Trump administration and witnessed first-hand how the media downplayed the most important stories of the day in the White

House press briefing room that did not fit into the Washington echo chamber.

Both of us understand that our corporate media obsessively squabbles over issues which have absolutely no effect on people's daily lives whatsoever to obscure the core rot at the center of American society today. From impeachment to Donald Trump's latest tweet, the corporate media gins up controversy and abandons all objectivity whatsoever to fit their neoliberal pro-establishment worldview.

Contrary to some beliefs, nobody explicitly designed this system. In all likelihood, no news director ever decided to black-out coverage of Bernie Sanders and Andrew "John" Yang. Nobody instructed Rachel Maddow and MSNBC to push the most outlandish Russia-gate conspiracy theories for three years and to undermine their credibility for years to come. An undertold part of the story of Ukraine-gate was how media organs, desperate for some drama and intrigue after Russia-gate fizzled, pumped the new whistleblower complaint and foreign intrigue so much that Democrats obediently followed their calls to impeach.

And while these outlets were wasting your time exhaustively telling you about the latest reason why the other team is so uniquely awful, they failed to tell you that neoliberalism is collapsing around the world in a 1914-style shift in the international order. They didn't have time after all—Donald Trump's latest Twitter insult is just *SOOO* much more important. As our friend Kyle Kulinski says: they spend all day every day trying to "How dare you, sir!" Trump to death.

The media's egregious behavior stems from the same problem—oligarchical control. Oligarchs, after all, are by definition a unique few with intersecting corporate and political interests. Increased corporate control of the U.S. news media has turned the industry responsible for covering the powerful into one that is instead their propaganda arm.

Nothing better illustrates this problem than Jeff Bezos' ownership of *The Washington Post*. The world's richest man outright owns the second-most powerful newspaper in the entire country and if you suggest that this is tied in any way whatsoever to that newspaper's coverage, YOU are the conspiracy theorist. The entire media world had a collective meltdown when Bernie Sanders dared suggest that maybe Bezos owning the second-most important media outlet in the country wasn't the healthiest situation for our democracy.

Reporters, cable news pundits, and editors are not hired by corporate media companies because of their skill for fairly reporting the news. The skill oligarchs value the most is instead knowing where the lines are, which stories are helpful to their agenda, and which stories are *sensitive.*

By and large, these are smart people and they respond to incentives. They went to the best schools, they scrapped their way up through competitive environments, and they know *exactly* who owns the company. They know that the best way to get on TV is to talk about Russiagate, they know that saying "Trump voters are racist" will get them booked more often on MSNBC, and they see their bookings decline if they dare to so much as mention Andrew Yang or say anything remotely positive about Tulsi Gabbard or admit that Bernie Sanders could win.

None of this is to make excuses for these individuals or companies. Just because nobody within the system designed it to be intentionally evil doesn't mean that the results still aren't catastrophic. The people who control hundreds of billions of dollars in media no longer have any credibility with the working class of this country. Their increasing role is to push a woke pro-corporate view of the world to stop people from waking up to the real class differences and existential threats to our society.

Suffice it to say, we've tried to take a different tact. We don't tow the line. We don't fixate on elite obsessions just because the rest of the media does. Of course, we get things wrong and we aren't perfect, but we try to be honest and to always view power skeptically. In other words, if you're the type of person who thinks that the nation's opioid crisis is more important than impeachment, then our show *Rising* may be for you. If you're the type of person who wants to be fair to a mass working class campaign that has defied all political expectations, then we may be your people.

The good news is that the elite media has become so brazen about their agenda that most people have woken up. A majority of Americans told Pew Research they have little or no trust in the media and 61 percent say that the news media fails to cover important stories.[5] Younger Americans have grown up in a particularly devastating age. They've watched the media lie to the American public about Weapons of Mass Destruction in Iraq, they watched as they ran cover for the banking industry after the financial crisis, and they watched as they refused to critically cover President Barack Obama when he sold out the working class who voted for him in favor of corporate interests.

More recently, the entire world literally saw ABC News Anchor Amy Robach admit on a leaked tape that her network quashed a story on the degenerate exploits of Jeffrey Epstein because they were apparently more interested in getting a sit-down interview during the marriage of Prince William and Kate Middleton. They watched how NBC got scooped on their own reporting about Harvey Weinstein because they feared his money and power and didn't want to compromise their access to Clinton world, which had of course been funded in part by Weinstein's donations.

Younger Americans know more than anyone that the news media is misleading them, and that's why they made a generational collective decision to just turn them off and seek truth elsewhere. The runaway success of our show and so many others on YouTube is a direct indictment of the mainstream media. Millions of Americans have abandoned traditional gatekeepers of information in favor of those who do not bow to the whims of their corporate masters.

The essays you'll find in this chapter touch on all of these themes. You'll hear how the media has dismissed the candidacies of Bernie Sanders, Andrew Yang, and Tulsi Gabbard while relentlessly pushing impeachment. We lay out how the media has failed to accurately explain to the American public why Donald Trump won the presidency and detail the rotten core of the American economy. The common thread throughout all of these essays is

5   https://www.usatoday.com/story/news/nation/2019/07/23/pew-study-american-trust-declines-government-media-and-each-other/1798963001/

the total lack of understanding of the problems that the American working class faces, and the media's shameless safeguarding for masters of capital in our society.

Why Bernie Sanders Is Right About Corporate Media

Saagar Enjeti

Bernie Sanders and Donald Trump committed an unforgivable sin to the U.S. media. They said the quiet part out loud. They pointed out the obvious truth that Jeff Bezos's ownership of *The Washington Post* influences that paper's coverage. For pointing out this truth, they were both viciously attacked by the so-called arbiters of truth in the mainstream media.

As I've said many times on the show, anyone with a functioning frontal cortex knows that ownership of a media organization influences the coverage you get from that outlet. Yet *The Washington Post* has the audacity to call Bernie Sanders a "conspiracy theorist" and Trump a threat to the free press for drawing a relationship between their coverage of him and their ownership.

If this outrage was limited only to *The Washington Post* it would not be as pernicious to society. The problem is that every single journalist in elite media also wants to work for *The Washington Post*, which means that they too will either stay silent on this obvious conflict of interest, or they will actively attack those who dare to tell the truth because it is a direct threat to their future career trajectories.

This essay seeks to outline not only why Bernie Sanders and Donald Trump are right to highlight Jeff Bezos's ownership of *The Washington Post*, but to show the tangible real-world benefits that such ownership provides oligarchs within our society. This real-world benefit comes from the unwitting (and at times witting) alliance of neoliberals operating within media institutions who push an agenda that benefits the bottom line of the richest and most powerful in the United States.

August 14, 2019

Senator Bernie Sanders is under fire from the political press for daring to link negative coverage of his campaign to Amazon CEO Jeff Bezos's ownership of the flagship newspaper in the U.S., *The Washington Post*. CNN called it "dangerous", and *The Washington Post*'s executive editor Marty Baron called it a "conspiracy theory," noting that Bezos has allowed his newspaper to "operate with full independence."

The Hill
August 13, 2019
Headline: Washington Post editor calls Sanders claim about campaign coverage a 'conspiracy theory'
By Morgan Gstalter

I have no reason not to believe Marty Baron, and I personally know many journalists at *The Washington Post* who are tenacious, well-sourced, and relentless. But we don't talk enough in this country about whether it is okay for the world's richest man to own arguably the most prestigious chronicler of politics today, nor do we consider the societal implications of such a dynamic. Let me give you a good non-political example: how are readers and the public supposed to be certain that the journalists at *The Washington Post* aren't self-censoring while reporting about a new 10-billion-dollar contract dispute between the Pentagon and Amazon. Or, perhaps, they're being too diligent about reporting the story, which may ultimately undermine Amazon's competitors and lead to it getting the contract.

Either way, billions of dollars are on the line for Jeff Bezos, and it's rather convenient for him to own an institution that can shape the entire narrative around the deal when the going gets tough. See what I mean? It gets very sticky very quickly, and you can have all the best practices in the world without raising legitimate questions in the minds of many Americans.

The Washington Post
August 1, 2019
Headline: After Trump cites Amazon concerns, Pentagon reexamines $10 billion JEDI cloud contract process
By Aaron Greg and Josh Dawsey

I don't believe that Bernie Sanders meant that Bezos was deliberately sending *The Washington Post* after him; the Senator explained as much in an interview with CNN. What he was highlighting, however, is the coziness of so much of the media industry and those that stand the most to lose from real populism. The best part about this system for so many in power is that nobody is technically paying or influencing you to exactly say or do something. Instead, the system is designed to incentivize promotion, coverage, and advancement of those that truly believe in policies that disproportionately benefit moneyed interests.

Some of you might be curious why someone on the right like me even cares about this. But woke corporate power is just as much of a threat to the right as it is to the left. Just go take a look at the most vicious opponents of President Trump and Bernie Sanders—there's a lot of overlap there. President Trump is right to call out the 'Amazon Washington Post,' and so is Bernie Sanders.

A Unified Field Theorem of Media Bias

Krystal Ball

One of the most consistent themes in elite media coverage of the 2020 Primary is just how ideological and biased it is. Of course, they swear up and down that they are just reporting the facts, nothing but the facts, but somehow the facts seem to get a little garbled somewhere along the way. While certain candidates are treated with kid gloves, hailed as the next big thing, touted as surging when the polls show no such thing, others are subjected to quite a different kind of treatment. They may be inadvertently left off of graphics. Polls in which they are performing well may be considered "outliers" so that they don't have to be covered or discussed. Alternatively, news outlets will "accidentally" misstate their numbers entirely, or ascribe their higher polling numbers to other more favored candidates. Powerful quotes are misattributed, tiny downward poll movements elicit calls for the candidate to drop out, nefarious motives are assumed for anything and everything.

It's not hard to see the common thread connecting the candidates who are beloved and the ones who are ignored at best and smeared at worst. Of course the elite media prefers centrists, but there's actually more to it than that. See for example the many glowing profiles of Elizabeth Warren, particularly the hot takes on her selfie lines. (One actually made the case that Warren's selfies put her in the league of renowned abolitionist, Frederick Douglass. For those of you who watch *Rising,* you can imagine how hard my eyes are rolling and Saagar chuckling as I read that line.) Warren is not as left as Bernie, but she's certainly from the progressive wing of the establishment-friendly part of the party.

On the other hand, the candidates who are treated with scorn are ideologically distinct. Sanders is consistently left, Tulsi is ideologically heterodox with some more conservative and some more progressive positions, Yang mixes left with libertarian, and Marianne embraces her own form of spiritual progressivism. The following essay was written just as the primary began to heat up in the late summer of 2019 and it became clear just who the media darlings and villains were going to be. It's my attempt to offer a unified field theorem of which candidates will be hated by the media and why.

September 6, 2019

In August of 2019, CNN displayed a curious on-screen graphic. It looked ordinary enough—a listing of top candidates in a national Quinnipiac poll. But, a closer look exposed a glaring omission. Rather than listing the sixth place candidate Andrew Yang, who was then polling at three percent, they skipped right over him and instead included Beto O'Rourke, who had only garnered one percent in the same poll. In isolation, you could be forgiven for chalking this omission up to a simple error. Some overworked producer just overlooked Andrew as they threw together yet another graphic for the day's show. Unfortunately that explanation becomes completely untenable when considered alongside all of the many other errors and omissions that seem designed to remove Yang's existence from the Democratic primary entirely.

One of Mr. Yang's supporters, Scott Santens, keeps track of these slights on Twitter. Each may seem minor but together they paint a damning picture. Another example from the same day included an MSNBC graphic, this time with a national late-August Monmouth poll, which also excluded Yang. That time, Yang rounded out the top seven, just a single point behind media-favorites like Buttigieg and Booker at three percent. The rest of the field followed at two percent or less. Santens also documents oddly unbalanced graphics that seem to include just enough candidates to get the media favorites in but exclude Yang. There was a time when an MSNBC anchor, apparently totally unfamiliar with Andrew's groundbreaking candidacy, had to apologize after calling him "John Yang" while a graphic displayed the same. Not wanting to miss out on the fun, CNN gave "John Yang's" wife a new name. This treatment has naturally extended to the debates, where moderators routinely call on him less and ask him stupid questions like: 'What would you say to Putin if you were elected President?' In fairness, though, all of the candidates routinely get asked stupid, obvious or otherwise pointless questions at the debates. Harder to explain is the fact that at an MSNBC-hosted debate, Yang wasn't called on until more than 30 minutes in and ended the night with a mere six minutes and change of speaking time, less than half of the struggling and low-polling Cory Booker.

It was after this debate that the candidate himself decided to speak out, boycotting MSNBC and demanding an apology. If all these examples aren't enough for you, Axios pointed out in September that at the time, while Andrew was sixth in the polling averages, he was fourteenth in terms of the number of articles written about his candidacy.

In other words, yes, all candidates complain about the media, but the media has demonstrably worked overtime to try to erase Yang's entire candidacy. And he is not the only one who the media appears to either disregard or hold in active contempt. Without fail, every candidate who has come from outside the Democratic establishment or who has dared to question the Democratic establishment has been smeared, dismissed, or ignored by the media.

There's Tulsi Gabbard, the Hawaii congresswoman who in 2016 resigned from a leadership position in the Democratic National Committee in protest over their treatment of Bernie Sanders. She dares to challenge the bipartisan pro-war foreign policy consensus and has been continually smeared as unpatriotic. *The Daily Beast* accused her of being "boosted by Putin apologists," citing as evidence that three out of her tens of thousands of donors had tangential links to Russia. Keep in mind that this woman being accused of having foreign allegiances is an Iraq War veteran who, to this day, serves in the Hawaii Army National Guard. Ms. Gabbard had the distinction of being the most Googled candidate in both of the first two debates. The media, however, has shown little interest in understanding why her pro-peace message might garner support.

I've talked quite a bit about existing media bias against Bernie Sanders. In one egregious case, a Washington Post "Fact-Check" found that Sanders had accurately cited academic research but managed to give him three Pinocchios anyway. It's almost impressive how they manage to pull this stuff off. And Marianne Williamson, while definitely off the beaten track for a presidential candidate, is also an incredibly accomplished woman, with seven *New York Times* Bestsellers to her name, and decades of activism under her belt. Perhaps it would be interesting to hear more of her thoughts on national healing and reconciliation, rather than just casting her as a weirdo and mocking her for a tweet about the power of prayer — a lifestyle many, if not most, Americans subscribe to.

These candidates occupy different poll positions and have wildly different approaches, styles, and philosophies. Andrew the cheerful prophet of doom, Marianne the spiritual healer, Tulsi the teller of hard-truths about American imperialism, and Bernie the...Bernie. But they have something important in common: they don't fit the mold. They aren't in the club. They defy the rules.

Asian techies are supposed to develop the latest AI, not lead the revolution to put humanity first. Democratic women veterans are supposed to burnish the party's hawkish cred, not doggedly pursue diplomacy and engagement while calling out the American war machine. Spirituality is not supposed to be mixed with politics on the left, even though religion is fully weaponized by the right. And with Bernie, well, septuagenarian democratic socialists who are not fashionable in any way are not supposed to be rockstars with the kids or top-polling presidential contenders. Rather than deal with these contradictions—contradictions, by the way, which have clearly fascinated the public, judging by Google and Twitter trends, fundraising numbers, and crowd sizes—it's easier to mock, smear, or ignore.

Not only do these candidates not fit the mold, but they also, in their own ways, represent threats to current holders of power. Marianne and Andrew didn't come up through politics, and they owe absolutely nothing to Washington or the Democratic Party figureheads. Tulsi dared to defy the Hillary coronation, so she *definitely* can't be trusted. Senator Sanders, though, is obviously the ultimate threat to the Washington neoliberal establishment. I recently asked him whether he represented an existential threat to the Democratic Party and he told me point blank: "In some ways I am, and that is that I want to transform the Democratic Party."

Sanders matches his critique of the party's corporatism and business as usual approach with an unmatched grassroots army and fundraising base. He has his own base of power that wants nothing to do with a DC cocktail party. When you are a threat to the political establishment, you are inherently a threat to the careers of political journalists who rely on access to that political establishment. There may not be an edict coming down from on high to destroy those candidates who threaten the system, but there are natural defense mechanisms that kick in: strange graphics that just happen to leave you out, "fact-checks" that don't seem to arrive at any facts—coverage that vacillates from total blackout to wild smears. Candidates who don't conform may be exactly what the country needs, but they are precisely what the media scorns.

Ronan Farrow And Why The Media Covers For the Powerful

Krystal Ball

"Is this really worth it?" According to Pulitzer Prize-winning journalist Ronan Farrow, that was the question posed to him by NBC News President Noah Oppenheim with regards to his reporting on Harvey Weinstein. Not, "How many women has this predator victimized?" or "What resources can we give you to nail this monster?" Nope, for the President of NBC News, the operative question was apparently a simple cost-benefit analysis. "Is this really worth it?"

That question, right there, really tells you everything about how all of these news organizations are run. They would like us to believe that they are simply choosing the most worthy stories to pursue without fear or favor, but their actual conduct makes such a notion an absurd joke. When it came to Weinstein, the executives at NBC News instead reportedly weighed things like their personal relationship and shared class interests with Harvey Weinstein. They weighed how much money he had to spend on lawyers and private investigators. They likely weighed whether their access to Hillary Clinton, a significant beneficiary of Harvey's largesse, might be impaired. Ultimately, weighing all those concerns, the bosses at NBC decided to kill the story. By their calculation, one of the most important works of journalism of the era was apparently not "really worth it."

Ronan's reporting provides such an important window into how these organizations are actually run, what concerns they actually weigh, and who and what matters to them. It translates directly into how they run their election coverage as well. As they ask themselves that question: "Is it really worth it?" the answer will be quite different when they are considering negative news about their Democratic establishment allies on whom they depend for Washington insider access versus negative news about those outside of their establishment circles. It's costless to attack Sanders. It's always "worth it." But it's quite a different calculus when you're talking about Elizabeth Warren or Joe Biden. Of course, in the end, they're not really fooling anyone, which is why trust in the media has eroded so deeply and why Trump's false cries of "fake news" have rung true for so many people.

October 10, 2019

In my former colleague Ronan Farrow's book, *Catch and Kill*, he paints a quite sinister portrait of NBC News, where according to Farrow, a culture of harassment, self-interest, and elite coddling ultimately led the organization to spike the groundbreaking Weinstein story. The story has turned into one of the most significant feats of journalism of our time, sparking the #MeToo movement and earning Ronan a Pulitzer Prize. At the time, NBC News President Noah Oppenheim said, "The notion that we would try to cover for a powerful person is deeply offensive to all of us." In fact, that "notion" is precisely what Farrow claims to expose.

Here are just a few of the bombshell allegations in this new book. First of all, Ronan reports on a new rape allegation against Matt Lauer. A woman who was working with him in Sochi for the Olympics tells Ronan that the star anchor anally raped her. Lauer denies the charge and claims their affair was strictly consensual. I know nothing about these charges against Lauer, but I can tell you that even I was aware of rumors of improper behavior about him during that period.

In addition, Ronan reports that NBC News Chief Andy Lack pressured multiple subordinates for sex and retaliated against them when their relationships soured. Lack denies those allegations as well.

At the center of Farrow's book is how Harvey Weinstein tried and was ultimately successful in getting NBC News to kill the story on him. Ronan had to hire his own camera crew and take the story to *The New Yorker* in order to get it published. Weinstein played the fellow elite card. He relentlessly called the big bosses Phil Griffin, Noah Oppenheim, and Andy Lack to pressure them. According to Farrow, here's how one of those calls with Andy Lack went:

> **Weinstein**: "It was the '90s. You know? Did I go out with an assistant or two that I shouldn't have, did I sleep with one or two of them, sure. We all did that."

> **Lack**: "Harvey, say no more. We'll look into it."

You can tell from the "hey bro" demeanor of these calls, these guys were buddies. They were part of the same club. And according to Ronan's reporting, Lack did in fact sleep with an assistant or two that he shouldn't have. Ronan also reports that Weinstein attempted to weaponize Lauer's misconduct in order to kill the story. Weinstein allegedly threatened to reveal information about Lauer that had been gathered by the folks over at the National Enquirer. NBC denies that they were ever presented with damaging material about Lauer. But a key implication of Ronan's reporting, is that NBC's own widespread problems made it much harder for them to hold other powerful men to account for similar misconduct.

In another telling exchange, Oppenheim told Ronan that his Weinstein reporting and a related recording would force them to "make some decisions ... like, is this really worth it?" Think about the implications of that statement. Weinstein is rich and powerful with a lot of friends and plenty of money for good lawyers, not to mention private investigators. It'll be uncomfortable at parties. Other people in the club may be mad. The cost-benefit model of news analysis will always favor taking down the powerless who can't fight back, over the powerful who have the money and the connections to put up a fight.

Clinton world is also implicated here. At the time when he was reporting out the allegations against Weinstein, Ronan was also working diligently to secure an interview with Hillary Clinton on foreign policy. Secretary Clinton's publicist Nick Merrill sent him a gem of an email explaining that the "big story" Ronan was working on was "a concern for us." In other words, drop the story on Weinstein or no interview. Weinstein had been a big donor to Hillary's campaign. It ultimately took her an eyebrow-raising five days to issue any sort of statement following the initial *New York Times* reporting on Weinstein's sexual misconduct.

The whole thing is a sordid stew of elite coddling and cowardice. It's also an extreme parable of how the news process too often works. News isn't judged just on its newsworthiness. It's filtered through a prism of elite solidarity and class solidarity and institutional self-preservation. Matt Taibbi in his book *Hate Inc.* writes about the proliferation of news stories that punch down at the local restaurant or marginalized citizens. They're just so much easier to take on. It's more difficult, costly, and uncomfortable to challenge those with power, the banks, or the big corporations or the Harvey Weinstein's of the world.

While Ronan's book is ostensibly about NBC and how his former news outlet came to lose out on one of the most significant stories of our time, it's really about so much more. He paints a picture of the ugly underbelly of one news organization, but the same story could have easily played out at any of the major news organizations. I have talked quite a bit about how the news media reflects the interests and tastes of the affluent. Ronan's book may reveal an absurdly extreme example of that maxim, but the truth is that the news media covers for powerful people every day.

ABCs Coverup For Jeffrey Epstein Spotlights The Dangers Of Corporate Media

Saagar Enjeti

No single story highlights the utter failure of elite institutions in America more than that of Jeffrey Epstein. Epstein's use of wealth to basically use the commanding heights of American culture to cover up his decades of pedophilia explictily highlights the epic failures of our media.

Epstein used his possibly ill-gotten gains in order to purchase relationships with the most powerful people in the world, from American presidents to members of the British monarchy. These powerful people in turn exerted pressure on media companies which sought to expose his disgusting crimes, allowing him to prey on young girls for decades longer than he should have been able to.

Epstein's manipulation was best on display after the leaking of internal video from ABC News which showed Good Morning America anchor Amy Robach admitting that her network's' leadership quashed a story revealing his exploits alongside British royal family member Prince Andrew.

The video not only revealed how corporate media covers for the most powerful in our society regardless of how hideous their crimes, but is also revealing from the fallout...or lack thereof. To date the only person who has been fired because of this incident is the low-level producer within ABC who clipped the video and saved it to their internal system.

No executive has been made to answer for this cover up, the normal media reporters who would hound the executives at ABC for a statement have decided by and large to stay silent, and business as usual continues at the news network owned by the Disney corporation. One wonders just how much powerful people across the world have to lose if a full account of Epstein's crimes were to ever materialize.

This essay was written immediately after the ABC tape leaked and is an attempt at tying the threads of the Jeffrey Epstein broader coverup to the corporate structure which props up our media today.

November 6, 2019

In November, Project Veritas released explosive leaked footage of ABC News reporter Amy Robach lamenting, on a hot mic, that ABC killed a story she had developed surrounding alleged Jeffrey Epstein victim Virginia Roberts leveling accusations on tape years ago not only against the now-dead financier, but implicating member of the British royal family Prince Andrew. She also had detailed reporting on connections between Epstein and former president Bill Clinton.

> Robach: *"I've had this interview with Virginia Roberts. We would not put it on the air. Um, first of all, I was told 'Who's Jeffrey Epstein? No one knows who that is. This is a stupid story.' Then the Palace found out that we had her whole allegations about Prince Andrew and threatened us a million different ways. Um, we were so afraid we wouldn't be able to interview Kate and Will that we, that also quashed the story. And then um, and then Alan Dershowitz was also implicated in it because of the planes. She [Virginia Roberts] told me everything. She had pictures. She had everything. She was in hiding for 12 years. We convinced her to come out. We convinced her to talk to us...it was unbelievable what we had, Clinton (Bill), we had everything. I tried for three years to get it on to no avail. And now it's all coming out and it's like these new revelations and I freaking had all of it. I, I'm so pissed right now. Like every day I get more and more pissed cause I'm just like, oh my God, we, it was what, what we had was unreal. Other women backing it up...Brad Ed-*

wards, the attorney three years ago saying like, like we, there will come a day when we will realize Jeffrey Epstein was the most prolific pedophile this country has ever known. And I had it all three years ago."

Robach's horrifying story contains all the same ingredients of a similar alleged NBC News coverup of Harvey Weinstein's story, detailed by enterprising journalist Ronan Farrow. The British Royal Family began exerting immense pressure on ABC News, who was desperate at the time to score an interview with Will and Kate. In other words, ABC News bosses allegedly killed a story into a sexual predator to preserve their relationship with the powerful.

These are the type of behind-the-scenes revelations that rivet a nation. We all know these types of things happen daily but are rarely captured so vividly on film. ABC News is, of course, denying the story in some language you may find familiar. First, they released a hostage-like statement from Robach, who was allegedly "caught in a moment of private frustration" and that she "could not obtain sufficient corroborating evidence" to meet their "editorial standards." She also claims in the statement that nobody at ABC ever told her to stop investigating Epstein.

ABC News released their statement side-by-side, saying that Robach's reporting did not meet their standards to air and that they never stopped investigating the story. This is complete B.S. Robach lays it out in the video: her bosses told her "nobody knows who this guy is," in relation to Epstein. Does anyone seriously think that's not a clear order to stand down?

ABC's explanation is strikingly similar to the one NBC used as a pathetic excuse for not airing its Harvey Weinstein reporting; that it "did not meet their standards to air." Yet, what is more newsworthy than an alleged photo of a member of the British Royal Family with his hands wrapped around a 17-year-old girl at the residence of a known sexual predator?

Every single one of us knows why ABC News did not run this story and why NBC News killed the story into Weinstein. They wanted to preserve their relationships with the powerful. This type of behavior can be perfectly exemplified by a dinner party at Epstein's New York mansion in 2010. According to *PageSix*, former Bill Clinton staffer and current ABC star George Stephanopoulos once had dinner with Prince Andrew to discuss the upcoming wedding of Kate Middleton and Prince William. This was two years *after* Epstein was given his sweetheart deal by Florida prosecutors and was still required to register as a sex offender.

Also attending the dinner party? The host of CBS Evening News, Katie Couric, CBS's Charlie Rose, Woody Allen, and Chelsea Handler. I think we all know the answer to that. They were cozying up to power and solidifying the base Epstein had used and would continue to use for years in order to cover up his horrific crimes.

Page Six
December 6, 2010
Headline: Prince Andrew talks of royal joy over Prince William's wedding
By PageSix.com Staff

This story is important for many reasons. Not only does it demonstrate beyond a shadow of a doubt that our corporate media giants not only defend the powerful when it comes to things that may hurt their collective bottom lines but that, when push comes to shove, they will stop at nothing even to cover up a whole host of their crimes.

The important thing to remember is what media outlets like ABC News and NBC News choose to cover while they're quashing stories into Jeffrey Epstein or Harvey Weinstein. Story selection is the most pernicious form of media bias. What they choose to ignore often matters more than what they choose to show you.

New York Times Bias Has Very Real World Implications

Saagar Enjeti

One of the hallmarks of the Trump age is the decision of media institutions like *The New York Times* to mortgage all of their credibility in favor of a blatant political agenda. Previous essays have outlined how this political agenda is hand in glove with the interests of the most powerful people in the United States.

A politically dubious story about Justice Brett Kavanaugh quickly fell apart in *The New York Times* after prompting several presidential candidates to call for his impeachment. The facts undermining this call for impeachment were disputed in the very book that *The New York Times* was running an excerpt from.

The mechanics of media bias are revealed in this essay by demonstrating what exact information gets printed in The Times and the types of people who populate our elite media institutions. As Noam Chomsky so aptly pointed out in his book Manufacturing Consent, people who would report the truth do not get the opportunity to do so because they would never be hired at elite media institutions in the first place. Whether you are a Kavanaugh fan or not, everyone should be concerned about the media's willingness to ignore facts and twist the truth.

This essay seeks to explain the actual mechanics of media bias by focusing on this single botched story and to demonstrate what havoc a biased media has wreaked onto our political system.

September 17, 2019

This month, *The New York Times* admitted an error in a pivotal story about Supreme Court Justice Brett Kavanaugh, which led to several Democratic candidates calling for his impeachment. The botched story drew harsh criticism from the right and the left, and it's the latest in a series of embarrassing mistakes for the so-called paper of record.

The Hill
September 16, 2019
Headline: New York Times issues correction on Kavanaugh story
By Alicia Cohn

The error began on Sunday when the paper published a book excerpt from two of its reporters, Robin Pogrebin and Kate Kelly, who are the authors of a new book on Kavanaugh. They alleged to have found a sexual misconduct allegation against Kavanaugh while he was a student at Yale University. The paper purported to have witnesses and even said that Congressional investigators had been made aware of the claim at the time of now-Justice Kavanaugh's confirmation hearing.

There is just one problem. Until Mollie Hemingway at *The Federalist* got her hands on a copy of the book, nobody knew that the book itself noted that the alleged victim did not recall the incident in question. In other words, some people are saying something happened between two people, and the two people involved in the incident don't actually recall it. However, that detail wasn't added to *The New York Times'* story until two full days after running it.

By that time Senators Elizabeth Warren, Kamala Harris, and others called for Kavanaugh to be impeached for lying to Congress about an incident that, if not outright false, has some serious doubt around it. I'm sure some readers probably still want to see Justice Kavanaugh removed from the bench, but the key thing to realize here is how much of a disservice that *The New York Times* has done us all with its handling of this report.

The biggest and most obvious form of bias in the mainstream media is about story selection and story response. Can you imagine if *The New York Times* had made a similar error about a Democratic Supreme Court Justice? Dean Baquet would once again have to haul himself in front of a town hall of his peers in order to explain how such a terrible error happened, and how he would ensure that such an incident never happened again.

Anyone worried about media bias should be very concerned about this incident. For those who may not be conservative, just think about the next time that *The New York Times* gets something obviously wrong about Bernie Sanders or any other progressive. They could care less what you think, so long as they can still get booked on MSNBC, talk to the same party insiders, and protect their status inside elite circles within New York and Washington.

The New York Times demonstrates that many of the organizations tasked with exposing those in power have become co-equal branches of the powerful overlord elites intent on pushing this country in a singular direction. What too many of my friends on the right don't understand is that these institutions aren't uniformly left; they're a specific type of Democrat who is the ally of the woke warrior and not necessarily the class warrior.

I want to emphasize again that nobody at *The New York Times* or *The Washington Post* ever got a memo telling them to write a story a certain way. But that's not how media bias actually works. Only the people who already subscribe to a certain ideology would ever get hired at these institutions. If you happened to go against the grain, you would never be allowed to work there in the first place.

Any candidate or cause that dares to question their class consensus gets targeted and becomes the victim of "unfortunate errors" and other debacles. In the meantime, our race to the bottom in media continues at an ever-faster pace.

How Much Damage Has MSNBC Done To The Left?

Krystal Ball

My former employer, MSNBC, is the most trusted news outlet among self-identified Democrats. Democrats, by and large, view that cable news net as an ally helping to educate them and to prosecute the case against the Republicans. There's only one problem: MSNBC is no friend of the left. Whereas FOX News was explicitly conceived as a sort of news arm of the Republican Party, MSNBC was not. It's simply a profit-driven venture that happened to stumble on a lucrative business model by catering to a more left-leaning audience.

Never has this dynamic been more apparent than in the Trump era, when in search of ratings, MSNBC has been happy to indulge the most insane of the Trump-Russia conspiracy theories, obsessively focusing their coverage on his alleged collusion to the near exclusion of all else. That means rather than focusing time and journalistic resources on the many ways Trump has failed to live up to his promises, they instead obsessed for years over every meeting anyone who ever met the President had with someone with a Russian last name. No one could have done more to hand this President sufficient ammunition to effectively neutralize every attack, real or legitimate, against him.

If you watch the mainstream press you'll be led to believe that Trump supporters are some cult-like monolith of unthinking worshippers. I won't deny that there's a certain loyalty there which is typical of those who have aligned themselves with something controversial. There's a higher psychological price to be paid to admit you were wrong when the initial position you took involved risk. Personally though, I certainly haven't found your average Trump supporter to be any more or less dogged in their beliefs than your average #resistance warrior. You should always be skeptical of press claims which are self-serving, and the idea that Trump's people are mindless and unmovable is very self-serving. It provides a ready-made excuse for why all the days of breathless coverage and bombshell revelations never amount to much. A reason not to have to consider that maybe Russia and Ukraine obsession wasn't the best way to make the case against this President. A reason to avoid realizing that MSNBC is not your friend.

July 25, 2019

After watching seven straight hours of Robert Mueller's testimony, which at times felt more like nationally televised elder abuse, I could no longer avoid pondering the following question: How much damage has MSNBC done to the left?

This critique is not meant to be personal to the anchors and commentators there, many of whom I know, and some of whom are friends, having myself worked at the network for five years. Nevertheless, nearly all of those anchors and commentators got swept up in the ratings bubble that was feverish Russian conspiracy theories. At MSNBC, as in all things, systems and incentives are more important for analyzing any particular situation than individual personalities. Though, I dare say, some talent did drink more deeply of the Russia conspiracy waters than others. Rachel Maddow, you have some explaining to do.

It's not that I believe the Trump campaign's actions vis-a-vis Russia were acceptable or justifiable. The president's team sought to work with Russia, used Russian illegal activity to their own benefit, and then lied about the whole mess to try to cover it up. Those are the facts and it's a damning set of facts. *But* it doesn't feel like a damning set of facts when, for months, MSNBC built segment after segment—show after show—on building anticipation for a big reveal when we would learn the true depths of Trump's fealty and direct conspiracy with Putin.

In some of the most fevered speculation, primetime shows actually invited Jonathan Chait on to lay out his wild theory that Trump had been a Russian asset since 1987. Chait begins his analysis by acknowledging that Trump as a multi-decade-long Russian asset is "probably not true...but it might be." Characters like conspiracy gadfly Louise Mensch were also invited on. Mensch, through her Twitter account, often "reported" things like the false notion that Steve Bannon was getting the death penalty for espionage. This is not journalism. It's Infowars-style conspiracy theory. Every day, every hour, anchors, analysts and paid security state apparatchiks primed viewers to believe that soon we would know the devastating truth and the Trump administration would be doomed.

CNN and many other outlets are certainly not blameless in the hype machine. The Democratic Party was also plenty happy to engage in what ultimately amounted to silly speculation. But I single out my former employer in part because they were certainly one of the worst mainstream offenders. They're also the network with the most influence and caché among self-described liberals and Democrats. Their decision to jump off the Russia cliff has taken much of the party with them.

I'd also like to dispel the public perception that MSNBC is on 'team D' in the same way that FOX News is on 'team R.' They're not, and Democrats should not think of them as their allies. Like most corporate entities, MSNBC is a die-hard member of the Green Party—and I'm not talking climate here. Russia conspiracies were great for ratings among the key demographic of empty-nesters on the coasts with too much time on their hands.

This whole obsession and accompanying conspiracy mongering has done more damage to the Democrats' chances of winning back the White House than anything that Trump could have dreamed. Think of the time and journalistic resources that could have been devoted to stories that a broad swath of people might actually care about. Health care, wages, the teacher's movement, whether or not we're going to war with Iran.

Following Mueller's anemic and befuddled testimony, I

actually heard a pundit on *All In with Chris Hayes* opine that independent women in middle America were going to be swayed by what he said. That is almost as bonkers and lacking in factual basis as that time Mimi Rocah said Bernie Sanders wasn't pro-woman because that was what 'her feelings' told her. Rocah, a former federal prosecutor with no political background, is, of course, only an analyst at MSNBC because of her role in leading viewers to think that, any day now, the Southern District of New York is going to bring down Trump and his family.

Most of the wild Russia conspiracy theorizing fell apart when the Mueller report was released, but one key element of the storyline remained: Mueller the hero. The white knight who would come riding in at the last moment to convince those independent middle America women that Trump was the crook and the scoundrel that we said all along. Needless to say, after today's testimony, the white knight rides no more.

Of course, in many ways, Trump really is the crook that we said all along. But by trying to make the spectacular case, Democrats and the media set the bar unimaginably high and made Trump's actual corruption, broken promises, and casual cruelty seem ordinary by comparison.

MSNBC Thinks The Left Needs Them.
We Don't.

Krystal Ball

The Trump era has revealed much. One of the things that it has most clarified is just what the ideological bent of the nation's premier "liberal" network actually is. MSNBC, which was accidentally forged into a left-leaning network by opposition to George W. Bush and the Iraq War, has now come full circle, welcoming the very Bush-era neocons it once scorned — complete with former security state torture implementers — into the fold. It's not entirely clear to me whether this new posture is an evolution or really just a clearer picture of what the network has always been about. Either way, progressives have fled the network in drove seeking out alternative media brands instead.

The 2016 Democratic primary had already exposed quite a lot about the wing of the Democratic Party that MSNBC was playing to. Their clear bias for the DNC-anointed candidate said quite a lot. But I thought perhaps an even more significant moment came during this current Democratic primary, when Andrew Yang found his treatment by the network to be so egregious, he actually announced a boycott of the network. This would have been an unthinkable option for anyone seriously vying for the Democratic nomination until very recently. Also consider the context here. Yang is not known for being hot-tempered or capricious, but he is known for his willingness to speak with anyone, regardless of ideological view, who's up for a more or less honest conversation. That the supposed "liberal" network could not meet this relatively low standard is an embarrassment. That one of the most interesting and certainly the most unexpected breakout candidate of the Democratic primary could publicly announce that they don't need MSNBC at all, is a cable news catastrophe.

November 25, 2019

After having been completely slighted in two different debates, presidential candidate Andrew Yang finally put his foot down with MSNBC. In a series of tweets, Yang laid bare the network's dismissive and contemptuous treatment of him stating:

> "Was asked to appear on @MSNBC this weekend - and told them that I'd be happy to after they apologize on-air, discuss and include our campaign consistent with our polling, and allow surrogates from our campaign as they do other candidates'. They think we need them. We don't."

In a second Tweet, he justified his boycott further, saying:

> "They've omitted me from their graphics 12+ times, called me 'John Yang' on-air, and given me a fraction of the speaking time [in] over two debates, despite my polling higher than other candidates on stage. At some point you have to call it."

In other words, he brought receipts and the internet responded. #BoycottMSNBC trended on Twitter. In a very real sense, this was a watershed moment for the network. I don't think you can possibly overstate how big a deal it is for a serious contender in the Democratic primary to boycott the network that is most directly associated with the Democratic Party (and lazily referred to as "liberal" or left-leaning). It took courage for Yang to do this, and I'm sure it was extremely uncomfortable for a network that seeks to be *the* destination for a left-of-center America. However, Yang's move simply revealed a fissure that's been a long time coming.

The extent to which MSNC was ever really a creature of the left is questionable. At worst, it's always been a corporate capitalist enterprise that happened to stumble on Keith Olbermann and found that rage against the Bush administration made for a successful business model. Disgust for the neocons was a unifying force on the left and Keith was fiery and unapologetic.

The Obama years were slightly more complicated. That's the era when I was at MSNBC, and there was a whole lot of uncritical team-blue-Obama cheerleading that I admittedly participated in much too often. I spoke out on TPP and Keystone and the banking bailouts, but I was particularly trusting on the national security state and in buying the binary narrative that the Republicans were always generally bad and the Democrats were always generally good. But the Republicans conducted themselves poorly enough during those years to be a fairly unifying force as well.

The larger fissures really started to show during the 2016 primary. I kicked off the primary season with a monologue begging Hillary not to run because she was too closely tied to the elites who had spurred massive inequality. Some of you have probably seen it. Let's just say it wasn't received very well.

Ironically, MSNBC's own Steve Kornacki was maybe the first to predict the rise of Bernie. Before Bernie started having massive crowds and before the millions of donations flowed in from across the nation, Steve intuited that there was a desire for an alternative to Hillary and that the early primary states, especially Vermont-neighboring New Hampshire, were good for Bernie. But beyond Steve's work, the network never took Bernie seriously or covered him like a real challenger to Hillary.

NBC News president Andy Lack, who, full disclosure, is the guy who fired me, arrived in 2015 with a mission to ditch the liberal lean of the network. I guess it was uncomfortable for him and the other execs at cocktail parties to be associated with a network where labor unions might be mentioned positively and trade deals negatively. They excised pro-working class voices like Ed Schultz from the network. Ideologically centrist journalists from NBC News were brought in to take over for more left-leaning opinion shows. Executives went on a right-wing hiring spree of Bush-era neocons.

This lineup change positioned MSNBC perfectly for their current Trump-era incarnation, where they are essentially a mouthpiece of the national security state, purveyors of the elite-approved critique of Trump, centering around his unseemly personality and disrespect for "norms," and a bastion of the discredited neoliberal establishment.

They have gone all-in on a fundamentally anti-progressive narrative that spends all day every day fixated on excuses for why Hillary lost to the guy they promised would lose (that would be Comey and Russia-gate and Ukrainegate as an extension of Russia-gate). Moreover, they fixate on "Trump is bad" as the end-all-be-all of political analysis. Everything that is going wrong in the country and the world is centered on him and him alone, because to evaluate the underlying circumstances that brought us Trump would be to question the undying wisdom of that very same Democratic elite. The people who created the underlying conditions that brought us Trump definitely do not want to talk about the underlying conditions that brought us Trump. They have devoted the network to the lionization of Bush-era neocon Republicans and the national security blob including Nicole Wallace, Steve Schmidt, John Brennan, Malcolm Nance, and more.

Meanwhile, the network is absolutely shameless in the way it covers the three anti-establishment candidates, Bernie, Tulsi, and Yang. Every interview with Tulsi must include the obligatory "Assad apologist" question and conspiracies about her running third party or being a Russian asset. *In These Times* recently did an analysis of Bernie's primetime coverage on the network, and found that he is mentioned a third as often as Biden, and far more negatively than any other candidate.

In These Times
November 13, 2019
Headline: MSNBC Is the Most Influential Network Among Liberals—And It's Ignoring Bernie Sanders
When the networks primetime pundits do cover Sanders, they cover him more negatively than Elizabeth Warren and Joe Biden.
By Branko Marcetic

Guys like Donny Deutsch spend every morning talking about how Trump is the end of the republic, but then proclaim that they would vote for Trump over Bernie. That's without even mentioning the amount of industry-approved right-wing talking points that are regularly rolled out to attack progressive priorities like Medicare-for-All and the Green New Deal. MSNBC is not liberal and it's certainly not the left. There is nothing intellectual or principled or progressive about simply reflexively opposing Trump and worshiping the Republicans who oppose him, all while they refuse to reckon with their own role—from deregulation to zombie Reaganism to the Iraq war—that helped create this mess. The one thing they all have in common—the neoliberals and wealthy executives and Bush neocons—is a vested interest in pretending that everything was fine before Trump and everything will be fine after Trump.

That brings me back to Andrew Yang. Some of you will object to calling him progressive. That's fine. But there's no doubt that his ideas fall outside of the spectrum of pre-approved acceptable ideas. There's no doubt that his candidacy challenges those in the party who want to maintain control over the acceptable pathways and trajectories to power. If Andrew Yang can be successful—already besting senators, governors, and congressmen—then the party is exposed as the impotent, hollowed-out shell that it actually is.

Don't get your hopes up that Andrew's apology from MSNBC is coming any time soon. After all, why apologize when they are doing exactly what they intend to do? The Trump era has been clarifying in many ways. Every real progressive now knows that MSNBC is not their friend.

As Yang put it so cuttingly: "They think we need them. We don't."

The Media's Working Class Blind Spot

Krystal Ball

There's one thing you should understand about elite media if you are going to make sense of any of the editorial choices they make, stories they decide to pursue, obsess over, or ignore completely: their product is not meant for the working class. Remember, the news business is a business with a target market. The target market for most elite media and for the advertisers who fund them, is the mostly white, upper middle class. That means all coverage is tailored to their particular interests, needs, and desires.

This predilection is exacerbated by the fact that newsrooms are increasingly populated with a monoculture of those who come from relatively privileged backgrounds, attend prestigious schools, and live in a few metro super regions. The end result is that the working class is either ignored completely, caricatured, or demeaned, their lives and concerns virtually ignored.

Understanding this dynamic explains so much of the manifest blind spots in our political coverage. The consistent underestimation of Bernie Sanders is the most obvious current example. Political reporters don't personally know the Amazon warehouse workers and WalMart workers and teachers who have sent him in $10 and $20 by the thousands so they completely dismiss the reality and potential of his movement.

The consistent misunderstanding and mischaracterization of Trump's support is another perfect example. In 2016, in spite of the massive rallies, flood of small dollar donations, and evident energy around his campaign, the reality of his support didn't penetrate the social circles of elite media journalists so they couldn't believe that it was real. Once he was elected and it became undeniable, rather than grappling with what his election says about the media or the establishment Democratic Party, the instinct has been to either make excuses (Comey! Russia! Facebook!) or to blame the voters (Racist! Sexist! Cultist!). That's not to say that these excuses don't contain a grain of truth or merit, but they've also served as a crutch to let the media and Democrats off the hook for their own failures.

This blanket broad brush painting of Trump supporters has led to continued errors in coverage and in Democratic Party tactics. After all, how can you win people back, when you have no understanding of what motivated them in the first place? How can you win people back, when you harbor active contempt for them? After the October 2019 debate, I noticed a curious item of post debate coverage that I thought perfectly and hilariously illustrated this media blindspot.

October 23, 2019

Following the October 2019 Democratic primary debate, Saagar and I — but mostly Saagar — relentlessly mocked the debate moderators for wasting all of our time with a lengthy exploration of "surprising friendships."

Near the end of the debate, the following question was posed to each of the candidates: "Last week, Ellen DeGeneres was criticized after she and former president George W. Bush were seen laughing together at a football game. Ellen defended their friendship, saying, 'We're all different, and I think that we've forgotten that that's okay," debate moderator and CNN host, Anderson Cooper, asked the candidates, "So in that spirit, we'd like you to tell us about a friendship that you've had that would surprise us and what impact it's had on you and your beliefs."

This question, of course, was explicitly designed to elicit *pablum paeans* to a lost, but not forgotten, halcyon bipartisan era of civility. Sure, George W. Bush lied us into war, sanctioned torture, destabilized the entire Middle East costing hundreds of thousands of lives and trilliions of dollars at a critical juncture in our nation's history, but at least he wasn't mean to people on Twitter. But perhaps Saagar and I were too harsh because it turns out that, for at least some journalists, this hard-hitting friendship question was actually quite revelatory.

In particular, *The New York Times* was stunned by Andrew Yang's answer that his "surprising friendship" was with a for-merly-Trump-supporting truck driver named Fred that he met on the campaign trail.

Keep in mind, the fate of truckers is a central parable and concern in Andrew's campaign. Anyone who has listened to a single Yang speech will have known this. Andrew wrote about truckers and the threat to their livelihoods by automation in his book, *The War on Normal People*. He talks about it at every chance, tweets about it regularly, and he has spoken to us about it in our interviews with him. Polling shows this focus has paid off. He has in fact garnered some support among the working class, and with truckers specifically who are worried about automation and ap-preciate Yang's concern for their livelihoods. As a result, Truck-ers for Yang is a group that *exists.* As of September, only Sanders and Warren had received more donations from self-identified truck drivers.[6]

As someone who is covering this election to include An-drew Yang's candidacy — despite the noticeable media black-out — it's not in any way surprising to me that Yang is friends with a truck driver. But the hard-nosed journalists over at *The Times* were immediately skeptical of Andrew's friendship claim and so they did what journalists do — they asked the *hard ques-tions.* Here's what *The New York Times* had to say in their debate "analysis":

> "At Tuesday night's debate, moderators asked the Dem-ocratic presidential candidates about a friendship that might surprise people. Andrew Yang said he'd befriended a trucker and former Trump supporter named Fred. The two men drove around in Fred's truck for hours, Mr. Yang

6   https://www.opensecrets.org/news/2019/09/sanders-vs-warren-who-has-more-working-class-donors/

said, and eventually, Fred came around to support Mr. Yang for the nomination. My colleagues — and probably more than a few people watching at home — were skeptical about this 'Fred.' Was Fred about as real as Pierre Delecto?"

That's right, those at *The New York Times* didn't dig in on Biden's dubious claims that he was central in setting up the Consumer Financial Protection Bureau, or to any of the centrists' claims that working with Republicans to get things done was within the realm of possibility. Instead, they had to get to the bottom of "Fred the Trucker." I'll also award extra points here for fitting in a boomer-friendly "Pierre Delecto" joke!

The piece gets even better when it turns out that they never had to reach out to Fred: he noted their skeptical coverage during the debate, and took it upon himself to reach out to *The Times* in order to prove his existence. He explained to the credulous *Times* reporters that Yang "connects with people who feel like they don't matter or count." Well, that seems pretty simple to understand.

Here's the bottom line. *The Times'* shock and confusion over "Fred the Trucker" are perfectly emblematic of their complete ignorance toward the working class in America, which includes the white working class. You can imagine their caricature of a deplorable, racist, "build-that-wall" white working-class American completely disintegrating as they talk to Fred.

This false idea of the white working class as racist, brainwashed Trump supporters is convenient for both the media and the Democratic Party. It keeps them from having to ask hard questions about why the white working class would throw their support behind the historic party of plutocrats and a reality show billionaire like Trump. It also keeps them from asking hard questions about why so many Americans don't participate in the political process at all: it's not their fault—it's the "dumb, lazy, racist voters."

That's not to say that racism isn't a real barrier for working-class solidarity. It is. Racism has been cynically exploited for decades by Republicans to hold together their overwhelm-

120

ingly white coalition. It has also been exploited by Democrats who know that if they can just appear less racist than the GOP, then they won't ever have to deliver material benefits for working-class people of color. But painting the massive, complicated group of people in middle America with a broad brush is offensive, absurd and extraordinarily counterproductive.

Here's the other thing: *The Times'* shock and confusion also completely exposes how little they understand about what drives voters. The idea that what the white working-class Trump voter really wants is Amy Klobuchar or Pete Buttigieg-style moderation is completely insane—not to mention belied by all the data. The fact of the matter is, the candidates with the most crossover Trump support are the most radical and most anti-establishment: Bernie, Tulsi, and Yang. That little factoid has apparently never registered for the elite media or the Democratic establishment. It doesn't factor into their bullshit "electability analysis" or their debate-night optics chatter about *Pistol Pete*.

This absurd and vacuous analysis of the mythical white working-class voter is maybe best illustrated by David Brooks' October column entitled *"Why Trump Voters Stick With Him."* Rather than speaking with actual human beings about their Trump support, he simply imagines the musings of a hypothetical "flyover man." One of many resident neoconservatives at *The Times*, Brooks' amazing thought experiment is just another amazing example of how disconnected those in the establishment are when it comes to understanding how everyday Americans think. If you really grapple with the fact that 70 percent of Americans are furious with the political establishment, their embrace of more transformational politics should hardly be surprising.

And that brings us back to Yang, who seems to understand the anger of that 70 percent more than most. You see, it turns out Fred isn't the only truck driver public in his support of Mr. Yang. Another truck driver named Dennis shared his thoughts in a Facebook video uploaded by the Yang campaign. Speaking directly with Yang, here's how he explained his support:

> The fact is, you're actually worried about the little guy. You know, you're actually worried about the truck driver, you're actually worried about that man or lady answering

the phone, or the fast-food worker that nobody is ever going to get up on any kind of political platform and talk about...They just don't seem to remember that, hey, it's the little guy like us, the blue-collar worker, that built this country."

So maybe that friendship debate question wasn't entirely useless. Sure, the public may not have learned much. But for at least a few moments, journalists had to grapple with the fact that Trump voters are actually human beings capable of complexity and not just thought-experiments in a David Brooks column.

Bloomberg Exposes Oligarchical Control Of The Media

Saagar Enjeti

Everyone hates the media. Most of us have our own personal reasons, be it ignoring a particular candidate, whitewashing stories of immense importance, or obsession with stories that the working class of this country doesn't care about but the elites do.

The more difficult task that confronts us is discovering just how things got this bad. How did we come to a place in this country where our media is a mouthpiece for the powerful instead of a necessary fourth estate of government? The answer is a deeper structural flaw of the American economy which encourages combination within industries of immense importance to our democracy.

Media companies have become intrinsically linked with the powerful corporations that they are supposed to hold to account. The three largest broadcast networks in this country are owned by Comcast, Disney, and Viacom, respectively. The second-most powerful newspaper in America is owned by the world's richest man. *The New York Times*, which was once relatively independent when financed by advertising revenue, is now beholden to elite subscribers who will tolerate no dissent from their outlook of the world.

How is any media company supposed to fairly cover the issues that affect the American oligarchy when they are directly beholden to it? This applies more so to issues of coverage for the working class of America for whom attention and assistance are most likely to come at the very expense of these oligarchs.

Aside from Bezos's ownership of *The Washington Post*, however, no oligarch has been more brazen in his control of a media company than Michael Bloomberg. Michael Bloomberg is the ninth richest man in the United States depending on the day. When he decided to run for President he flat out ordered his company not to investigate him during the race, and then his newsroom decided to extend that privilege to all of his Democratic compatriots.

This essay was written the day after *Bloomberg News'* decision and outlines the practical and moral dangers of a media increasingly owned by oligarchs.

November 25, 2019

Michael Bloomberg is many things, but we must all at least thank him for exposing the true danger to our democracy that corporate media poses. In late November, *Bloomberg News* Editor-in-Chief John Micklethwait sent a note to staffers outlining how they will deal with their boss as he threw his hat in the presidential ring. Many took notice of the fact that they would suspend their editorial board, but another stray line caught my eye.

Micklethwait writes that the news organization will "continue our tradition of not investigating Mike" and that, in keeping with their policy towards competitive financial companies, that they will not investigate any of Bloomberg's rivals. It sounds on its face like the ethical thing to do, but think about how much of a gift that Michael Bloomberg's corporate control over a major news organization grants him.

It is difficult to describe how much of an in-kind political donation it is to have one of the largest newsgathering organizations on the planet vow to not investigate you while you're running for president. Now, you might say, 'But they're not investigating anyone else!' Well, um, that's a very bad thing too!

They're supposed to be investigating candidates: that's literally their job as reporters.

But this isn't just about Mike Bloomberg; all *Bloomberg News* did was say the quiet part out loud. We live in a time where oligarchs of immense fortunes control media companies to shape the public environment in order to benefit their business. One of my favorite reactions to *Bloomberg News'* announcement was the indignation and surprise from Washington Post journalists like Paul Farhi, who called the statement "extraordinary" on Twitter. Do you know what is more extraordinary? That Jeff Bezos, the world's richest man, owns *The Washington Post*, the second-most powerful newspaper in this entire country. At the same time, the entire news media insinuates that when Donald Trump or Bernie Sanders link that fact to the coverage of a particular news organization, that they're outlandish conspiracy theorists and putting the institution of journalism in some sort of danger.

When Jeff Bezos paid 250 million dollars for *The Washington Post*, in effect what he purchased was the right to stop the second-most powerful newspaper in the United States from investigating his company, Amazon, and even better—that he could use that company to hire people who share a similar ideology to his own, which benefits his bottom line. Even better for Bezos, every aspiring journalist in the country wants to work at *The Washington Post*.

All of them will think twice before Tweeting something negative about Bezos himself or investigating Amazon at a different news organization. What I just laid out is worth hundreds of billions of dollars in benefit to the market cap of Amazon and Bezos personally, just as *Bloomberg News'* neutralizing of negative coverage is a financial boon to the company's namesake.

As David Sirota noted on Twitter after Bloomberg's announcement, "Every reporter covering 2020 knows that if they write a story scrutinizing Mike Bloomberg they risk enraging a person who owns a sizable segment of the media job market. It is a tough situation for journalists and not a great dynamic for democracy."

Corporate control of the media has turned our contemporary politics into covering the needs and wants of the most powerful people in this country. Perhaps it's time we think about whether it's appropriate to keep letting them do so.

The Corporate Media Reckons With Their Years of Gaslighting

Saagar Enjeti

The elite media's corruption and disconnect from broader American society has been relatively fast in the making. Just a decade ago, the media's consolidation and control over the flow of information in the U.S. was a virtual monopoly with the internet merely nipping at its heels.

Just 10 years later, with the full solidification of the social media age, you would think they've started to learn their lessons as their relevance dwindles. Instead what has happened is that corporations and oligarchs have purchased media companies and turned them into propagandistic arms for their direct financial and social interests.

The good thing about naked propaganda, however, is that it enables the rest of us to confirm our long-held suspicions. My previous essay outlined how Michael Bloomberg's ownership of *Bloomberg News* and subsequent actions showed how oligarchs maintain control over our media.

This essay was inspired afterward by the reaction of the corporate media to the Trump campaign's decision not to credential *Bloomberg News* reporters in retaliation. Corporate media executives and reporters flocked to the side of *Bloomberg News* because all must maintain the illusion that they are not tools of the world's most powerful people.

Maintaining the illusion of objectivity is key to the corporate media's claim of monopoly on information distribution. As their audiences continue to shrink, they will only continue to gaslight the American public more through their powerful perches throughout the media. The good news is, the internet can fight back.

December 3, 2019

Consequences for the corporate media are finally starting to materialize. President Donald Trump's campaign announced that it would not allow any reporter from *Bloomberg News* to cover its rallies soon after Mike Bloomberg jumped into the race.

The Trump team's statement says, "*Bloomberg News* has declared that they won't investigate their boss or his Democrat competitors, many of whom are current holders of high office," adding that "since they have declared their bias openly, the Trump campaign will no longer credential representatives of *Bloomberg News* or other campaign events."

The move was not surprisingly met with whining from the cable news syndicate and couched as another attack by the president on the so-called fake news media, with *Bloomberg News* Editor-in-Chief John Micklethwait writing, "the accusation of bias couldn't be further from the truth. We have covered Donald Trump fairly and in an unbiased way since he became a candidate and will continue to do so despite restrictions imposed by the Trump campaign."

The New York Times Editor-in-Chief Dean Baquet even got in on the action, standing by *Bloomberg News*, calling it "one of the largest and most influential news organizations in the world," and adding that "we condemn any action that keeps quality news media from reporting fairly and accurately on the presidency and the leadership of the country."

Anyone with a functioning frontal cortex should snort at the idea that a media organization that bears the name of a Democratic presidential candidate can possibly cover their potential opponent fairly. *Bloomberg News* let the cat out of the bag in their original statement after the former New York Mayor's candidacy that it will "continue our tradition of not investigating Mike."

As I noted at the time, *Bloomberg News* said the quiet part out loud. They confirmed that when oligarchs own media companies there are massive conflicts of interest. It showed just how hollow so much of the sanctimonious preaching from the Brian Stelter types over at CNN is when they tell us that the people at *Bloomberg News*, *The Washington Post* and *The New York Times* are the fairest people on this earth.

It should chill you to your bones that the Editor-in-Chief of the 'newspaper of record' feels compelled to stand up for a news organization that has openly admitted their bias and is owned by the ninth richest man in America. Before our very eyes, we have one of the most transparent displays of the alliance between the news media and the moneyed elite in this country.

If you think conservatives are the only ones talking about this, check out what a familiar figure, Bernie Sanders, said to a classroom full of students about 16 years ago:

> "We have a handful of corporations like General Electric, Viacom—huge corporation owning CBS, Disney—huge corporation owning ABC, AOL-TimeWarner—huge corporation owning CNN, Rupert Murdoch's NewsCorporation owning FOX, NYPost, other media outlets all over the world...it is important to understand who owns what."

The man makes a good point. Recall that *The Washington Post* Editor-in-Chief Marty Baron said Sanders was peddling a "conspiracy theory" for suggesting that his negative coverage in the newspaper could be tied to the paper's ownership by Jeff Bezos.

That's what drives us all mad. People are smart—they know that when somebody owns something, they have influence over their product. They know that when a news organization literally bears somebody's name, that they're going to act in their favor. That's just how business works, and don't try and tell us otherwise. If they did that from the very beginning—told us the truth—then maybe people would have some trust left in the media. But no, they'll continue to gaslight us, and we'll continue to shake our heads.

III.
IDENTITY

Identity

The words "identity politics" get thrown around often—and not always by people with the best of intentions. Some would deny that racism and sexism are a reality in modern America at all. Some, in resistance to the 'woke' identity politics of late, are engaging in their own sort of bizarro-world identity politics, attempting to claim the mantle of most oppressed. These views are not ours.

However, we both have a deep skepticism of and contempt for those who would fixate on race and gender alone as a way to distract from the war-making and economic rigging that has proved so destructive for working class people of all races. We have nothing but disgust for those who would use identity as a wedge to divide natural allies from one another in order to maintain the status quo. After all, throughout American history, cynical politicians have weaponized race and gender to turn our working class citizens against one another, rendering them powerless. Because a true multi-racial working class coalition would be an unstoppable force, and no donor or multi-national corporation could stop them. The wealthy know quite well that they share class interests regardless of their race, gender or sexual orientation. Take a look at a Manhattan cocktail party and you'll see plenty of "bipartisanship" which strangely has the same interest.

The truth is that in an era where both parties have decided to center corporate interests, identity has been used to culturally pander to the working class so that you can keep screwing them economically. For those who hold power, it's relatively nonthreatening to embrace a type of change that would only go so far as to change the race or gender of the keepers of the status quo. The great American meritocracy, in which every little boy and girl can ascend to their rightful status, can be venerated and preserved if the only problem with it is bias of race and gender. Once you start thinking hard about class interests and start asking whether there's really anything so special about those people at the top of the meritocracy, that is ultimately a much more dangerous and potentially transformational view. What really threatens American elites isn't the notion that we need more women or more people of color with their boot on the throat of the working class, the real threat comes when people start asking why the working class should have a boot on their throat at all.

Of course, the way each party uses identity politics to placate the working class is different. Democrats and the left point to the dog whistles, exclusionary rhetoric, and voter suppression policies of the right and say, in effect, "Yes, the minimum wage hasn't been raised in a decade, including much of the time we were in power; yes, we participated in the gutting of welfare and unions and architected mass incarceration, yes, we bailed out our largely white banker friends and let minority home owners pillaged by subprime lenders drown, but you can't vote for those racist, homophobic people, can you? You have no choice but to vote for us."

Republicans and the right continue to hammer home that Hollywood elites and other cultural figures want to "change this country as we know it," which could be true, but then refuse to change their very own tax and trade policy which does everything to empower the people in our society who most seek to destroy their way of life.

While the bipartisan commitment to big money holds, the only battles that are fought are on the grounds of cultural signaling, rather than real economic change. There is genuine racism, sexism and hatred in this country—bigotry of all kinds. But what animates American politics right now is not a true desire to make America a place free of the systemic legacy of racist and sexist policies: what animates American politics is the desire for elites to cling to power, engage in rent-seeking behavior and hog all the spoils of the plutonomy for themselves. Identity politics is the sop thrown to working class people to keep them in line. It keeps us all running around yelling: "Racist!" and "Sexist!" and "Un-American!" at each other rather than noticing the way that we are all united in a shared struggle.

Identity politics has also been called into action to give a sheen of respectability to otherwise indefensible and morally bankrupt institutions. That's how you can end up with hellish dystopian situations like Wells Fargo sponsoring a luncheon with Black Lives Matter activist DeRay Mckesson called "From Black Panthers to Black Lives Matter: The Movement Continues." Remember that Wells Fargo was caught red-handed lying to their customers and opening unauthorized accounts and credit cards in their names! Shallow identity politics is why the mercenary consultant ghouls at McKinsey feel comfortable conducting and publishing research on how good diversity is for business, but probably are not going to be looking into how beneficial unions can be for workers.

For both of us, calling out the hollow, self-serving hypocrisy and cynical manipulation of woke identity politics has meant making a lot of people angry. One of the ways that identity politics works so effectively to repress dissent is by ruthlessly tossing the label of racist and sexist at anyone who doesn't toe the line. We utterly reject a line of thinking that would say you should be canceled just because you believe that the interests of the working class are best served by candidates who will fight on economic, structural and trade issues, regardless of the race or gender of that candidate.

We have applied this approach to our daily analysis of American politics and the 2020 campaign. We parse through the woke, identitarian rhetoric from the likes of Kirsten Gillibrand, Kamala Harris, Cory Booker and others on a near daily basis. These candidates all attempted to satisfy a change-hungry public with change in the identity of leadership alone, while preserving the brutal status quo for the multi-racial, multi-ethnic working class that is America. The right has been happy to exploit this situation as well, seizing on Democrats' pandering to convince the white working class that Democrats only really care about "those people," and that the Democrats, and specifically their 2016 nominee, seemed to leave the white working class behind. This clash of identity politics versus traditional cultural grievance leaves the working class with no real allies.

Over these pages, we have tried to dig deeply into the problems with identity politics and the people obsessed with this approach, and how they offer the wrong explanation for why we are where we are as a nation today. Identity politics alone has no room for critical analysis of trade deals, for unionization, for asking real questions about how our economy should function. Identity politics' lack of answers mostly comes from its complete incoherence. There is no better example of this than the freak-out amongst white feminists when Representative Alexandria Ocasio-Cortez endorsed Bernie Sanders. They blared from their Twitter feeds—*How could she?* There are other women in the race, how could *she* leave them destitute? They were bewildered by the notion that Sanders' policies were far more important than the hollow tokenism of the gender of the candidate.

In this next series of essays, you'll see many examples of the sheer incoherence of identity politics, particularly demonstrated by the complete erasure and hostility to presidential candidates Andrew Yang and Tulsi Gabbard. Both candidates successfully outlasted a number of more milquetoast establishment options, but have been outright ignored and smeared by elites within the Democratic Party and the media for nearly the entire stretch of the race so far, in spite of their trailblazing status.

The bias against Tulsi Gabbard and Andrew Yang stems from the fundamental messages of both campaigns. Gabbard's campaign is a heat-seeking missile directed at the bipartisan foreign establishment consensus on endless wars in the Middle East and failed trade policies. That consensus implicates far too many corporations and members of the neoliberal elite for it to be accepted in polite society, so they simply ignore her.

Andrew Yang's message is similar. His signature proposal of Universal Basic Income is rooted in a complete indictment of the entire establishment class's governance. Yang frequently discusses the failure of policy elites to grapple with rapid automation, for allowing the drug crisis to get out of control, and remaining completely out of step with the American working class. Unsurprisingly, this subversive message is not allowed to be heard by corporate media audiences.

It's also worth noting that the historic nature of Bernie Sanders' candidacy is almost never noticed at all. He's often dismissively referred to as another "old white man." It seems like the fact that he would be our first Jewish president, especially at a time of rising anti-Semitism, might be significant. It seems like the fact that he's the son of immigrants might be salient given the hot debates unfolding currently about immigration.

Other establishment politicians have also woken up to the superficiality of identity politics and frequently deploy such attacks for cynical political purposes. How else can you explain Cory Booker blackmailing the entire 2020 Democratic field into protesting the Democratic National Committee's debate rules by threatening to play the race card? Or Kamala Harris vacillating on the campaign trail for six months, losing traction, and then deciding to blame her failures on voters being too sexist or racist?

Identity politics fundamentally does not offer the United States a path forward through this time of immense social and political upheaval. The logical result of identity politics is endless racial and gender strife, which a multi-ethnic, multi-racial, multi-religious democracy cannot sustain. This is not to deny the reality of sexism and racism, which are real and deeply rooted. It's only to recognize that in an oppression Olympics, everyone loses. And that the only way to obtain a more equitable society across gender, racial, and religious lines is to start by confronting the corporate and financial power which cuts across all swaths of our society. In the following essays, you'll read many real-time takedowns of identity politics and its weaponization by corporate institutions which are only interested in exploiting the working class.

White Feminists Melt Down Over AOC's Bernie Endorsement

Krystal Ball

At the lowest moment of Bernie's campaign, when he had slipped in the polls, had his worst debate performance with a hoarse and raspy voice, and landed in the hospital after suffering a heart attack, Congresswoman Alexandria Ocasio-Cortez decided to endorse the Vermont Senator. There honestly aren't a lot of endorsements that really make any difference at all. AOC's endorsement is one of the rare few that actually matters. It was especially critical coming at the moment that it did, and helped to launch a resurgence pushing him into direct rivalry with Joe Biden for the top spot.

For those who pay the most attention to movements and ideology, AOC's endorsement made perfect sense. Of course, the activist bartender who started her term in office protesting outside Speaker Pelosi's office would back Bernie Sanders. But for those who cared more about AOC's identity as a young woman of color than her politics, her choice was shocking and confusing.

These are the same type of people who go through a ritual of pretending to be heartbroken every time a candidate of color drops out of the race, even though they themselves did not support that candidate. The same type of people who believe that you have to be sexist to choose Bernie Sanders over Elizabeth Warren. The same type of people who cling desperately to the belief that only white men support Sanders, in spite of all the evidence to the contrary. Honestly, their meltdown was a beautiful thing to behold. Is AOC sexist? Is she a Bernie bro?

Let me be clear, I am a feminist. But my aspirations are greater than hoping we can have more women as oil executives and hedge fund managers. As a woman, I support candidates who will create a system that provides dignity for all, rather than just changing the gender ratio of our oppressors.

In the essay below, I help our white feminist friends make sense of this new shocking development.

October 17, 2019

We are learning more details about Alexandria Ocasio-Cortez's endorsement of Senator Bernie Sanders for the presidency. According to *Politico*, AOC informed Senator Sanders of her decision while he was laying in a Nevada hospital bed, recovering from his heart attack. Here's campaign manager Faiz Shakir:

> "Think about the courage of this person who says, 'you know, I know what you just went through, but I have so much trust and confidence in you that you are the one who will fight the fight that I believe in. I'm with you. To hear that was like, 'wow.'"

'Wow,' indeed. I've explained before what AOC's endorsement would mean for her and for the candidate who has now received it. In part, I argued that endorsing Bernie at this moment, when the wind is at the back of his progressive rival (Senator Elizabeth Warren), would represent a profoundly important and courageous move:

> "Endorsing Bernie at this point is not a DC choice; it's a movement choice, an activist choice—a surefire way to get you disinvited from certain polite segments of DC society, and an unjustifiable gamble if you're playing for short-term-power-positioning. But, if you're commitment is really *to the movement,* if you believe that what the Democratic Party really needs is a good 'existential threat' and outright hijacking by the multi-racial working

class, then the choice is crystal clear."

It might be tempting to write AOC's endorsement off as the obvious choice. After all, she is a Justice Democrat. Her first run for office aimed directly at upending the establishment: a working-class Democrat who takes inspiration from the Sanders movement. She, herself, was a Sanders volunteer. But, in fact, it wasn't at all obvious that she would make this choice, at least not right now.

Just look at how the Working Families Party, a group with a mission statement that could be torn from the Bernie Sanders website, threw their support behind Warren this time. For AOC to back Bernie while the wind is at Warren's back is very much against her personal short-term political interest. After all, Warren has adopted the language of the movement, and embraced many of the policies that AOC champions, from Medicare-for-All to the Green New Deal. In doing so, Warren has given AOC plenty enough cover to sit it out if she wanted to. She could easily have chosen instead to throw her energy into defeating Biden rather than picking between the two progressive candidates.

AOC could have embraced the argument that Katrina van-den Heuvel at *The Nation* made in *The Post* when she argued that progressives ought to honor and embrace a truce between Warren and Bernie. In essence, either of these candidates is great, so let's just have a love fest for both of them and see what plays out.

AOC is rejecting all of that. She is picking sides. Picking sides implies, of course, that there are discernible differences between Warren and Sanders other than their gender—differences that matter enough to risk the wrath of a woman with a good likelihood of being the Democratic nominee. Differences that matter enough to risk upsetting a chunk of AOC's own followers who may have backed her because they loved seeing a young woman of color push out the old white guy, but are more invested in her identity than in the working-class populist movement she represents. For those AOC supporters, it was apparently very confusing for their girl-power champion to throw in with the old white guy over a progressive woman. For example, Jane Eisner, Director of Academic Affairs at Columbia Journalism School, in a now-deleted Tweet wrote: "I find it fascinating that women of color overlook female and minority candidates to endorse a white guy. Is 'identity politics' over? Is ideology more important than race and gender? Genuinely curious."

Well Jane, allow me to help you understand why AOC or Congresswoman Ilhan Omar or any other progressive would pick Bernie Sanders over Elizabeth Warren. I'm not sure anyone has argued what's at stake here better than Matt Karp. In his new piece in *Jacobin*, Karp lays out how the Democratic Party has rejected the politics of class solidarity in favor of embracing the professional elite. The results of this should be abundantly obvious: NAFTA, TPP, allowing union power to decline, banking bailouts, an embrace of woke virtue signaling to keep working-class minorities in the tent while providing nothing of substance in terms of their economic well-being. That's why Warren's upper crust fan base is in and of itself cause for concern.

Jacobin
October 14, 2019
Headline: Is This the Future Liberals Want?
By Matt Karp

As Matt points out, the Democratic Party—the alleged 'party of the people,' has won control of 20 of the wealthiest counties in the country. Every single one. Warren's coalition points to more of that; more sidelining of the working class. More embracing the tastes and priorities of wealthy liberals. More of the white working class identifying with the racist populism of the right. The Sanders coalition alone points the way towards a fundamental realignment of the Democratic Party around the working class. Here's Matt:

"An OpenSecrets review of campaign donations found that while Warren was naturally the top recipient among scientists and professors, Sanders led by far among teachers, nurses, servers, bartenders, social workers, retail workers, construction workers, truckers, and drivers. "Of all the money going to 2020 Democrats from servers — one of the lowest-paying jobs in the country — more than half went to Sanders alone. This is just what is required to challenge the power of the ultrarich: a politics that does not treat lower-income voters as a kind of passive

142

supplement for professional liberals, but one that can put the new working class itself at the center of the action."

And this is the choice that AOC has just made. It's a choice to center the working class.

True leadership isn't picking the winning side just before the election—the way that Warren did when endorsing Hillary in 2016. It also doesn't look like picking the person who happens to have the identity most similar to yours. True leadership looks like wandering in the desert of Democratic socialism, the way that Bernie did for decades when the DLC and corporatists turned us into the party of Davos, all while Bernie was alone on the national political scene. True leadership looks like backing Bernie Sanders when he's third in the polls—not because it's the opportunistic or smart choice, but because it's the *right choice.* True leadership means moving the hearts and minds of people to where they ought to be—not telling funders, pundits, and the media what they *want* to hear.

I've asked myself: Is AOC a true leader of character, or just someone who saw an opportunity to beat Joe Crowley, because of his arrogant, establishment bound complacency? But now we know the answer, and I am happy to say that the multi-racial working class has another champion to stand next to Bernie and fight the good fight.

Warren's 'Pink Scarf' Pledge Is Everything That's Wrong With Her

Saagar Enjeti

Beyond being a clear dividing line between more cultural-ly conservative voters and the social whims of white, college-educated elites, Elizabeth Warren's focus on divisive and fringe social issues is really just a cheap ploy to mask her questionable foreign policy views and distract from her reluctance to go all-in on key policies like Medicare-for-All.

Warren's decision to double down on these often head-line-grabbing races to see who can be most 'woke,' including in this section where I highlight her pledge to wear a pink Planned Parenthood scarf during the inauguration, has had the effect of pleasing New York and Los Angeles high society, while simultaneously making them feel comfortable by promising to work inside the established Democratic beltway.

All-in-all, Warren—who has not been able to pick up much working class support, especially in the way of donations, that Bernie Sanders has—has now resorted to the same failed tactics that doomed the likes of Kamala Harris, Julián Castro, and Beto O'Rourke. It just so happens that the working class is not worried about correct pronoun usage or the diversity of Hollywood films, but whether or not they'll be able to afford healthcare or have to ship their kids off to a faraway war.

In this essay, I explore how her co-option of these views to please Twitter reply guys have only watered-down the policies that should be front-and-center for a candidate whose slogan is literally "I've got a plan for that."

December 9, 2019

The grim future of an Elizabeth Warren presidency was put on full display this weekend in a series of deep dives into her campaign. The first began with a New York Times writeup on the fluid nature of the 2020 Democratic primary. The Massachusetts senator is apparently trying to contrast herself with Joe Biden, Pete Buttigieg, and Bernie Sanders by vowing to wear a pink Planned Parenthood scarf during her inaugural address and sprinkling her campaign stump speeches with reference to her gender.

I can't think of a more perfect symbol for how I've described Warren before as one whose presidency is almost certain to be marked by a failure to pass any substantive legislation on healthcare and financial reform, while issuing a flurry of woke social justice executive orders that will further rip the country in half along cultural lines. She is increasingly making it clearer that despite her rhetorical flourishes calling for Medicare-for-All, that she falls far closer to Joe Biden's theory of the case than she does a Bernie Sanders.

Check out this exchange with a voter in which Warren touts her public option choice for phase one of her healthcare plan, rather than the full transition:

Voter: From what I understand right now, Medicare-for-All right now has the supplemental, is that correct?

Warren: There is no Medicare-for-All, right now.

Voter: No, but Medicare, period. Medicare, period. Even in the French system, there is a supplemental, so what happened to that?

Warren: What we're putting together--it's complete healthcare coverage, for all the basics. It doesn't cover cosmetic surgery and things like that. It's to cover basic healthcare. Just so everybody knows, it includes vision, it includes dental, it includes hearing, and it includes the all-important long-term care.

Warren's entire healthcare plan is designed to reap the electoral benefits of calling something Medicare-for-All, all while basically proposing a robust public option. Remember, her so-called transition plan calls for Biden/Pete Care in the first three years of her presidency, before hopefully trying to pass a follow on to the bill in the third year of her presidency and somehow finding some time for immigration reform in there.

This is simply a fantasy. As I've said here before, she just doesn't believe that healthcare is the number one threat to the daily lives of the American worker. She was marked in the fights of 2008 and the financial crisis and believes institutional reform in that regard is what's needed. The problem, of course, is that healthcare is the number concern for Democratic voters, and that her transition plan reveals just how unserious about it she is, hence the massive drop in her poll numbers.

Warren's singular focus on financial issues highlights another grim feature of her presidency—the return to a largely neo-con, Washington-centric foreign policy. Journalist Zaid Jilani has commented on this show before that Warren appears to be running for Secretary of the Treasury rather than for Commander-in-Chief, especially given how little she talks about foreign policy. As Jilani so aptly put it, when you don't have anything to say on a topic, then it almost always just gets colored in by what the establishment wants when you're in power.

The Guardian
December 8, 2019
Headline: Donald Trump has destroyed American leadership - I'll restore it
By Elizabeth Warren

Warren let the cat out of the bag this weekend in a Guardian op-ed titled "Donald Trump Has Destroyed American Leadership, I'll Restore It." The op-ed grumbled about how Trump 'alienated' the NATO alliance, bashing him for meeting with Moscow and Pyongyang, and his questioning of international agreements that the U.S. is party to.

I've heard all of these same criticisms from *Morning Joe* panels or from CNN 'expert analysts' including the likes of war hawks such as Max Boot or Richard Haass at the Council on Foreign Relations. The entire op-ed is a dream for the cable news syndicate and could have been written by a foreign policy speechwriter for George W. Bush or Hillary Clinton. She writes, "As president, I will recommit to our alliances – diplomatically, militarily and economically."

The sheer normalcy of this op-ed is what should scare you. Normalcy means a default to the military-industrial complex, to the current system of subsidizing the entire world at the expense of the U.S. taxpayer and, above all else, lack of critical thinking about America's position in the world and how to use its military might to effect a major change.

All of this is to say is that Elizabeth Warren has thought very deeply about one thing: financial power in this country. I don't think any of us have doubts about that, but her total embrace of Women's March-style identity politics, playing political games on where exactly she stands on healthcare, and a neocon-lite foreign policy shows that she wants to please establishment Democrats so badly that she is almost certain to be co-opted by them if she were to ascend to the presidency.

Kamala Harris's Cynical Identity Politics Ploy

Saagar Enjeti

Kamala Harris's failure is a direct indictment of the identity politics-obsessed media that elevated her in the earliest days of her career. Her entire political ethos was founded on being a woman of color who touted Neo-Liberal economics. In other words, her candidacy was a way for Wall Street billionaires to justify the economic policies which benefit them, while feeling good about themselves by donating to a woman of color.

Kamala's gambit, however, only worked so long as she could show some sort of resilience in the polls. Her support evaporated as she equivocated on Medicare-for-All, backtracked on her own attack against Joe Biden on school busing, and repeatedly wavered on where she stood on issues of major importance to the Democratic primary electorate.

As the primary electorate saw that she generally stood for nothing, they began to abandon her in droves, to the point where she was behind upstart candidates like Andrew Yang and Tulsi Gabbard in the polls. Harris, of course, did not take the opportunity to take stock of her campaign to decide what issues she would like to make her case with.

Instead, the California Senator decided to use the media as a way to disseminate a false and disgusting message: that voters were too racist and sexist to consider her a plausible candidate who could beat Donald Trump.

This essay was written after Harris made these false and outrageous claims weeks before she ended her campaign for President. The most powerful weapon against those who are obsessed with identity politics is the electoral death it appears to deliver to those who rely on it as the foundation of their political life.

October 29, 2019

Senator Kamala Harris offered a well-reasoned and thoughtful analysis of why her campaign is failing in a new interview with Axios, acknowledging that her brand of moderate progressivism mixed with woke identity politics is the exact opposite of what the country wants right now. Just kidding, she blamed voters for being sexist and racist for not seeing her grandeur.

This is so wrong on so many levels. Kamala wants us to believe that voters who twice elected a black man named Barack Hussein Obama are racist. Furthermore, the Democratic electorate hoisted the first woman to a party's nomination in 2016, Hillary Rodham Clinton. Who, as Democrats always love to remind us...won the popular vote!

Her argument is facile on its face and it's insulting to millions of Americans. They're not backing Kamala Harris because she is not giving them a coherent reason to support her. She's not losing because of identity issues. Her campaign is failing because she doesn't stand for anything. In fact, her entire campaign seems predicated on standing astride the progressive and moderate left to appease exactly nobody.

A lesson of the 2016 presidential election is that voters need to trust you. They need to trust that you will actually fight for the things that you say you will. When push comes to shove, lobbyists are blowing up your phone, besieging the White House, and they buy off your best friend to make a pitch to you. That's why they took a chance on Donald Trump in 2016, probably one of the least conventionally electable people in our history.

Electability is a trust issue, and there isn't any real reason to trust Kamala Harris. She doesn't have bold solutions and she doesn't even offer voters the warm centrist return to 2012 that Joe Biden does. From the very beginning, she has shown us exactly who she is. Remember her spate of hard hearing a few months ago when a man referred to Donald Trump as "mentally retarded," and she laughed along with him, only to say she misheard the remark? I do.

That was the third time in a series of weeks that Harris claimed to 'mishear' something. If you'll remember, she pulled the same stunt after raising her hand in the June Democratic debate, indicating that she supported abolishing private insurance, only to later say that she 'misheard' the question. She then told reporters that she thought the moderators asked if she was willing to give up her own private health insurance.

In January, when CNN's Jake Tapper asked her a question during a town hall regarding stricter scrutiny of police shootings, she dodged, saying that as California Attorney General, she made it a practice of not weighing in on bills that concerned the matter. A Washington Post fact-checker analysis found that the claim was absolutely false.

Harris, in the early days of the primary, refused to actually commit to anything—and that is why she has monumentally fallen in the polls. As of late October, the RealClearPolitics (RCP) polling average shows Harris with just five percent of support. That's a mighty big fall from the 15 percent that she displayed in July 2019.

Things look even worse for her in Iowa. The candidate is putting up just 2.7 percent in the RCP polling average for the state, and in New Hampshire, she is at just 4.7% percent. Nevada? 4.5 percent. South Carolina? Seven percent. The highest she places in any early state or national poll is fourth place. Not exactly a 'top-tier' candidate anymore, huh?

When Will the Establishment Celebrate Tulsi's Diversity?

Krystal Ball

Nothing and no one is more vexing to the identity analysis of so much of the Democratic Party establishment than Tulsi Gabbard. Here she is, a veteran, a woman of color, first Hindu in Congress, youngest woman ever elected to the Hawaii state legislature. She checks every diversity and resume box we are supposed to look for in a candidate, and yet she is utterly hated by all the people who wring their hands about the lack of diversity in the Democratic field and pretend that they value diversity over ideology. Tulsi completely exposes the lie. They don't support all women of color, they support women of color who happen to uphold the neoliberal consensus and play nicely in the sandbox with the establishment.

That's why Tulsi was a rising star in the party, a darling of leadership, right up until she dared cross them. It's mind-boggling to realize she was actually a vice-chair of the DNC. They were happy to elevate and use her as long as she towed the line, but when she resigned from the DNC to support Bernie Sanders, she committed an unforgivable sin and will never be allowed back into the good graces of the Democratic establishment again. It was an act that took real courage, something that's rare to see in our politics, and Tulsi has paid the price many times over. She's paid the price again for committing heresy and daring to challenge the wisdom of Pelosi's national security state-driven impeachment. Her "present" vote was willfully misrepresented as cowardice when in fact it was anything but. How much easier would it have been for her to stick with the herd and vote "yes?"

Personally, I've been glad to have Tulsi's voice in this race, even when we've disagreed. She is principled and she has forced a conversation on foreign policy that the establishment never wanted to have, because they are complicit in launching our endless wars. The fact that it's a young woman of color triggering Hillary Clinton and the rest of the neoliberals is just an added bonus.

November 12, 2019

It is yet to be seen whether Hillary Clinton's endorsement will be at all helpful to the lucky candidate who receives it, but we can now say for certain that her anti-endorsement is tremendously helpful. Hillary's smearing of Tulsi Gabbard as a Russian asset has given her campaign a needed boost. In fact, a new poll has her at six percent in New Hampshire, putting her behind only the top four of Biden, Warren, Buttigieg, and Sanders. I'm still waiting for the neo-liberal celebrations that a woman of color is surging at a key moment in the race. By the way, top-tier Kamala managed only one percent in that same poll.

All of this means that Hillary not only gave Tulsi an assist in qualifying for next week's debate, she's also put her right on the cusp of the heightened December debate criteria. Tulsi now only needs one more poll at four percent or better to make it into that round as well. Keep in mind, of the approximately 379,000 candidates who ran for the Democratic nomination, only six have so far qualified for the December debate, so it's really nothing to sneeze at.

The accomplishment is made even more impressive by the fact that the media and the Democratic establishment have done absolutely everything they possibly can to destroy Tulsi. They've called her childhood 'weird,' accused her of being in a cult, questioned her patriotism at every instance, and insinuated that she's a white nationalist (which is weird since she's of Samoan descent, and was the first Hindu to serve in Congress). A typical example of the media's treatment of Tulsi was this exchange with *The View's* Joy Behar where, rather than ask about her policies, she instead has to explain why she's not a "useful idiot" and defend her decision to go on FOX News. It's all insinuation and guilt by association designed to leave you with an impression that the person in question is "toxic" or "problematic" without having to actually spell out why.

Again, there are of course valid critiques of Tulsi's policies, but this has been something else entirely. Ever since she dared resign from the DNC and back Bernie over Hillary, the establishment has been doing their very best to silence her. That she's managed to achieve some momentum in spite of all that shows you just how persistent she is and just how weak and feckless they are. They can't even crush one dissenter, and the other guy they loathe, Bernie Sanders, is the most adored politician in the country with the biggest crowds, most donors, and greatest enthusiasm.

There's some additional data of note in this poll as well, though. In New Hampshire, which has an open primary system, Tulsi does extraordinarily well with independents. In fact, a recent poll has her tied with Elizabeth Warren for independent support. In addition, she does very well with those who describe themselves as moderate or conservative. Tulsi's spot on the traditional ideological spectrum is kind of hard to peg, because her views are heterodox. At the same time that she's finding support with self-described conservatives, her supporters also tell pollsters overwhelmingly that their second choice is Bernie Sanders, who is, of course, the only true leftist in the race. The first thing that I would say about that is for many voters establishment versus anti-establishment is a more important barometer than the typical left-right spectrum—or maybe authentic versus inauthentic or principled versus pandering. We see it every day on this show. There is a massive group of Americans whose first commitment is to ending the disgusting bipartisan consensus of corruption, corporatism, and war profiteering that has so damaged our nation.

But there was something else that I found really amusing here. All day long, every day, we are told by *The Times* and *The Post* and CNN and MSNBC and everyone who ever goes on *Morning Joe* that to win we must appeal to moderate voters. We're told all the time that we should just throw our principles to the wind and back whoever has the "best chance" of beating Donald Trump. Well, here you go. Tulsi Gabbard is a candidate with genuine crossover support from Republicans and independents and moderates and conservatives. A veteran! A woman of color! The youngest woman ever to serve in the Hawaii state legislature! Come on, establishment, isn't she everything you told us we should want in a candidate? Yes, yes, I know you don't like her, but remember? We are supposed to suck it up and vote for the electable candidate, no matter what! Otherwise, you are a Twitter troll or a 'Putin puppet' or a traitor or whatever. And if you don't just automatically line up behind that person for unity's sake, then also you love Trump.

I'm still waiting for the establishment Democratic punditocracy to come together and announce their support of Tulsi. Judging by her crossover appeal alone, she may well be the most electable candidate. I'm still waiting for the elite media to switch from writing deep-dives speculating on Tulsi's 'nefarious motives,' to puff pieces on how she may well be a female Obama. Because just like CNN's Jeff Zeleny said about Pete Buttigieg, "both represent a fresh face, and are calling for change." I mean, both Tulsi and Obama ran on anti-war platforms. Obama didn't actually deliver on that, but whatever. Someone get a camera crew to New Hampshire, fast! Something tells me I shouldn't hold my breath.

Weirdly, and I know you're going to be shocked by this, it would appear that Tulsi's bipartisan and moderate support is being used as yet another way to dismiss her candidacy. Nate Silver — big numbers guy — wrote on Twitter: "Tusli (sic) is the choice of people who plan to vote in the Democratic Party but don't like Democrats and most of the things Democrats stand for."

Personally, I thought Amy Klobuchar was that candidate. But congrats to Tulsi on her campaign's upswing, and on her success in getting all the right people to hate her.

What Cory Booker's Whining Reveals About Democrats

Saagar Enjeti

Senator Cory Booker is a lot like Kamala Harris in many ways. He staked his political identity on a few too many profiles in the 2010s that he was the next President Barack Obama. He wrapped himself in the cloak of identity politics, solicited cash from Wall Street billionaires, and touted a similar neoliberal-friendly position from the Senate dais.

Unlike Harris, however, Booker's campaign has never really registered amongst voters anywhere. He has consistently lead the bottom of the polls despite early deep pockets and investments on the ground in Iowa. Despite his poor performance relative to anti-establishment candidates like Andrew Yang and Tulsi Gabbard, he has been given disproportionate speaking time on the Democratic debate stage and attention from the mainstream media. None of this has helped him.

The last time he was seen on the Democratic debate stage, he spent his final moments asking viewers to donate to his campaign and help him hit the threshold which would ensure his place there once again. The problem is his gambit didn't work and he did not qualify for the December Democratic debate.

Booker, unlike other candidates who accepted their lack of qualification and resolved to work harder, instead decided to force nearly every single other campaign in the race to protest the DNC rules on his behalf because it supposedly undermined diversity in the Democratic field.

This essay was written after Booker essentially black-mailed his more successful rivals into supporting him. It shows both the emptiness of identity politics and its power over so much of the left which, as I will expand on later in this book, will ultimately be the undoing of the entire project.

December 17, 2019

Senator Cory Booker is very upset that he won't qualify for future Democratic primary debate stages, so much so that he essentially forced all of the qualified rival candidates to come to his defense in a letter sent to DNC chairman Tom Perez. In the letter, they asked him to consider a rule change allowing candidates to make the stage if they make *either* the polling threshold *or* the requisite number of donations.

Booker's letter and public rhetoric is centered around the idea that the DNC rules are inherently discriminatory against *regular* candidates like him because billionaires like Tom Steyer and Michael Bloomberg are outspending him. He's gone so far as to say that the DNC's framework is having an "unintended consequence of excluding people of color."

The Hill
December 14, 2019
Headline: Booker leads other 2020 Dems in petition urging DNC to change debate qualifications
When the networks primetime pundits do cover Sanders, they cover him more negatively than Elizabeth Warren and Joe Biden.
By Tal Axelrod

There are problems with this. For example, a candidate of color named Andrew Yang had no problems hitting the polling qualifications or the number of donors. Furthermore, when a female candidate of color, Rep. Tulsi Gabbard, complained about the debate rules excluding her from the stage in the past (and for her treatment on stage), how many other candidates do you think rallied to her defense? Cory Booker certainly wasn't one of them.

One of the funnier parts about Booker's protests against billionaires being able to buy their way into the race is that he has the second-most number of billionaire donations in the whole field. As of December, the only person with more billionaire donors is Kamala Harris (who is now out of the race). She had also blamed billionaire spending for her lack of ability to continue her failed presidential campaign and subsequent fall from top-tier status.

Booker's gaslighting on billionaire spending, coupled with blaming structural racism for his failures as a candidate, is a disgusting and cynical canard meant to exploit real tensions in this country to extend his obviously failing presidential campaign. The American people and the Democratic electorate have had their say on Cory Booker, and they don't like what they see.

As journalist Zaid Jilani pointed out after Booker's protests, he is the only other candidate in the race who has a sanctioned super PAC running ads for his campaign. Even more, he even has an entire documentary on Netflix called 'Street Fight' and statistics from past debates reveal that he gets much more speaking time than he deserves on the stage relative to his polling position.

A guy named Andrew Yang, though, who nobody knew a year ago, still beat him to the stage. That isn't racism, that's democracy. Booker's washed up message of identity politics coupled with neoliberal economics has fallen flat on its face throughout this cycle as voters increasingly divide themselves along class lines and on theories of political change.

Every successful candidate knows this, and yet Booker was still able to get every single Democrat in the race to sign his whiny letter to the DNC? Anonymous campaign aides told *The New York Times* that candidates co-signed the letter, because if they didn't, they risked looking racist in the press or, at the very least, not supportive of people of color.

As I said yesterday, the electoral failure of the American left will be economic progressives kowtowing to woke identitarians. Bernie Sanders and Elizabeth Warren know exactly why Cory

Booker is not resonating with voters. There is not a serious bone in their bodies that believes 'structural racism' is what has kept Booker off the stage, and yet the idea that they signed the letter because of the perception of a racial slight by cynical woke actors like Booker is enough to sink you with the mainstream media.

Signing the letter in the grand scheme of things is a pretty minuscule act. People barely noticed it, but it matters. It matters because it demonstrates how much these candidates fear the woke identitarian left and why they will ultimately never be able to make the cultural concessions necessary to the right if they ever want to win.

A candidate I would actually respect is one who refused to sign the letter and told Cory to 'stuff it' and compete on the same playing field as everybody else.

Historic Election of Black AG Conveniently Ignored

Krystal Ball

In covering the off-year Kentucky statewide elections, I noticed a glaring hypocrisy. Somehow the national media forgot to celebrate the fact that Kentucky elected their first black Attorney General. Now I know very well why I didn't celebrate. The newly elected Attorney General was an aide to Mitch McConnell, whose values and ideology stand in direct opposition to mine. But shouldn't all of the people who lament the success of the "old white men" Biden and Sanders and pretend to be heartbroken when Cory and Kamala and Julián Castro fail in their presidential bids, shouldn't they at least pay some lip service to this historic and trailblazing achievement?

The fact that these identitarians don't celebrate Daniel Cameron reveals that they know just how hollow their commitment to identity politics really is. Slamming a candidate for characteristics they can't control is a simple way to try to dismiss them and preserve the status quo without having to actually deal with that candidate's arguments. On the other hand, elevating a candidate based on their identity can provide a progressive sheen to the status quo. A way to score all your good lefty points without having your own class interests, power structures, or cocktail circuit access threatened. A way to feel good about what a good person you are without actually having to commit to change a system that has allowed you to get yours.

The reckoning with this type of politics is only just beginning on the left as we grapple with the real legacy of the Obama years. It meant something to elect the first black President. I don't want to diminish that. But for the disproportionately black and brown and female working class, it would have meant more to have a President who fought for union rights, who helped middle class homeowners rather than standing by as their net worth was destroyed by criminal banksters, who didn't let corporations write his big Trans Pacific Partnership trade deal. The essay below is my attempt to expose the fact that even those who claim to ascribe to this type of politics do not actually walk the walk when it comes to valuing diversity over ideology.

November 8, 2019

Reporting on Election 2019, I found an interesting and underreported, genuinely historic result that occurred in Kentucky. I don't want you to miss it. For the first time in state history, Kentucky elected an African American to the post of Attorney General. Daniel Cameron, a former Mitch McConnell aide, became the first African American elected in their own right to any statewide office in the Bluegrass State; a state which is overwhelmingly conservative and 87 percent white.

I'm sure you were well aware of Cameron's trailblazing campaign, though, given the overwhelming celebration of his achievement by Democratic politicians, elite media and all of the folks who typically celebrate such identity-based achievements. Right? The white women who were horrified when AOC endorsed white man Bernie Sanders, the pundits who told us 'you have to be sexist not to support a woman,' and those who supported Kamala because of her identity as a black woman...they must have been elated by Daniel Cameron's victory, right? After all, if you can't see it, you can't be it. So, if the thing that matters is identity politics, surely Cameron's victory would be widely celebrated. So strange, that virtually no Democratic politician or elite media outlet said a damn thing.

Perhaps that's because identity politics is a thin gruel to be offered by the Democratic Party establishment, corporatists, and media elites in lieu of actually delivering anything of consequence. The lack of even one mention of Daniel Cameron's election shows you that they are well aware of just how shallow it really is.

I don't want to pretend that breaking race and gender glass ceilings is meaningless. It's not. I loved that the first president my kids knew was a black man. It does make a difference to see people of color and women in leadership roles. But if those people pursue the same racist, classist, elitist, crappy policies of their white brothers and sisters, well, it is not really *change we can believe in*, is it?

If you're an immigrant getting deported, does it matter to you that the deporter-in-chief is the first African American president? If you're in jail for marijuana possession or because your kids were truant at school, does it make a difference that it's Kamala Harris who gleefully prosecuted you? Aren't you delighted that Kellyanne Conway was the first woman to run a successful presidential campaign?

The truth is so obvious that it's embarrassing to state it. What you do, the policies you advocate for, and the people you help, matters. It matters a lot more than having equal and diverse representation in the advocacy and implementation of racist, anti-working class policies. It was Democrats who put in place the racist 100-to-1 crack sentencing disparity. Thanks, Joe Biden! It was Democrats who proudly destroyed welfare as we know it, Democrats who let the banksters off the hook so they could pillage African American and Hispanic communities with their subprime mortgages of mass destruction.

I could spend the next ten hours in a filibuster of woke Democratic hypocrisy on this issue. Tulsi Gabbard is a woman of color running for president. Why does she get no love from the left? It's because she doesn't step in line for the heterodox pro-war policies that have hijacked the party. If you're a millennial drowning in student debt, do you care that President Platitude Pete-the-millennial is the one who lets you keep drowning in that debt? If you are one of the parents of the 70,000 people per year that die of an overdose, do you care about the race, gender, or sexual orientation of the political coward who continues our racist and inhumane War on Drugs? Woke people need to wake up!

If the Democratic Party wants to win, then they should actually do something for the multi-racial working class instead of just changing the race of the so-called "leader" that runs palliative care for the working people in the giant hospice that both rural and urban America have become. And, by the way, if you don't believe the suffering of the white working class is just as real as that of the black and brown working class because they have "privilege"—people who have watched their jobs shipped overseas and their towns flooded with drugs and their young people sent off to die in war all by a bipartisan consensus — then you are just as heartless as those who would put precious immigrant babies in detention centers. This isn't an oppression Olympics where we get to stand in judgment of who is suffering the most. If Democrats want to be the party of working people, then they can't pick and choose which people. I want no part of the party centered around the professional-managerial class, throwing a bone of identity politics to the black and brown working class to keep them in the tent.

In November, Bernie joined Mehdi Hasan on his podcast Deconstructed. Mehdi asked Sanders if he would commit to choosing anyone except a white male as his Vice President. Bernie responded:

> "We have months to go. We will take a look at the best potential candidates out there. We're not ruling out anything right now...But this is what I will say, which is most important—trust me—that my vice presidential candidate will be a strong progressive."

'My vice presidential candidate will be a strong progressive.' It actually takes courage to say that: to say that the ideology matters first and foremost, and if it's a woman or a person of color, so much the better.

Democrats, you have a choice. Celebrate Daniel Cameron. Celebrate it when he prosecutes women for trying to get an abortion, celebrate rollbacks of worker protections and more mass incarceration because at least he's the right color. Or, get off this idea that identity politics are the only thing that matters. By their complete silence on Cameron's election, they have shown that obviously, it's not. Leave your identity politics at the door, and start evaluating people by the content of their character and their record, and not by some B.S. woke signaling that no one believes anymore—including, I might add, the demographic groups you are supposedly pandering to. Otherwise, prepare for another four years of Trump.

How Yang's Groundbreaking Campaign Changed Politics Forever

Saagar Enjeti

Andrew Yang is the perfect foil for identity-politics-obsessed elite Democrats. He's an Asian man who's never worked in politics before, defying political expectations and harnessing the power of the internet to give a voice to the often politically voiceless in our society.

There should be a million *Vogue* or *Vanity Fair* profiles written about him and how he's changed politics forever, and yet he has been the most consistently erased candidate of the 2020 campaign cycle. The reason is that Yang's message is fundamentally anti-establishment, which violates the central tenet of identity politics. Your identity is only celebrated if it does not upset the economic structure which benefits the wealthy over the working class.

Not only has Yang been ignored, but he has been attacked for not fitting the Asian stereotype that the elite media has prescribed for him. Yang's candidacy best demonstrates the canard that is identity politics and his success so far in the Democratic primary highlights how actual Americans refuse to balkanize themselves and instead reward people who seek simply to make their life better.

Yang's qualification for the Democratic debate was a sea change moment for American politics and should have been touted as a major victory for Asian Americans in the United States.

167

Instead, the media and establishment Democrats essentially implied he didn't count as a real person of color because there were no African Americans on the stage.

This essay came on the heels of Yang's qualification for the debate and defeat of Kamala Harris in her own home state. It seeks to contextualize his movement in the broader context of American history. We will look back and see that Yang's candidacy marked the beginning of a new age and his unintentional unmasking of identity politics will be a key part of his legacy.

December 11, 2019

On December 10th—joining the ranks of Joe Biden, Pete Buttigieg, Amy Klobuchar, Bernie Sanders, Tom Steyer, and Elizabeth Warren—Andrew Yang became the seventh and final candidate to officially qualify for the December 19th Democratic Debate.

It's worth pausing and taking stock of how extraordinary it is that Andrew Yang will be on that debate stage while media favorites like Kamala Harris, Cory Booker, Julián Castro, and other major U.S. political figures watch from home.

This extraordinary achievement represents a sea change in American politics that will come to define our political life in this next decade. Yang, an Asian-American businessman, has propelled himself to a long (but at least a real) shot at the highest office in the land, largely by harnessing the power of the internet and new media platforms, and most of all despite overwhelming bias coming from the mainstream media.

I don't agree with some of the fundamentals of Yang's diagnosis or his solutions to our country's problems. But what I very much respect is his willingness to break from the mold of what it means to run for president and who is "electable." His candidacy is, in many ways, a return to the fundamentals of democracy, where anyone is able to rise to the top of the political playing field if their ideas resonate with enough people.

The Verge
November 13, 2016
Headline: Donald Trump says Facebook and Twitter 'helped him win'
By Rich McCormick

Until Donald Trump in 2016, there was a traditional mold you had to fit before running for president. You had to have a team of policy professionals, you had to know the right party establishment brokers, and you had to kowtow to the wishes of billionaires in order to receive money and T.V. coverage. These established gatekeepers of power kept down heterodox voices until the internet came along. As Trump showed us all in 2016, Twitter is actually more powerful than cable news. When you ignore the establishment and harness a direct-to-people platform, the news executives ultimately have no choice but to cover it.

Because of the mainstream media bias against Yang from the very beginning, he understands this dynamic intrinsically and it has been a major factor in his success. Remember that his qualification for the debate stage comes after he and his supporters boycotted MSNBC, the major liberal establishment cable news organization in this country. Such a move would be anathema to almost any other candidate, but after he didn't sink in the polls, he actually raised 750,000 dollars in a single day and qualified to be on the next debate stage.

As the race narrows to Bernie Sanders and Joe Biden, figures like Yang are even more important on the debate stage. They force the leading candidates, the establishment, and the media to grapple with their ideas and push the Overton window of acceptable discourse. It's for this reason that Yang needs to step up his game in further debates and claim the stage and time that he and his supporters believe he deserves.

Are the moderators going to be biased in the amount of time they give him? Absolutely, yes. But that doesn't mean you just sit there and take it. You don't need to be as annoying as John Delaney to be pushy and insert yourself into the conversation. Nobody gives it to you, you have to take it. A strong debate performance from Yang, coupled with the undying love of his supporters, could very well result in shock finishes in places with a very independent streak like New Hampshire and Nevada.

Nationally, Yang has yet to break out of low single digits, and if he wants to win he needs to expand. For a while, his strategy appeared to be trying to sound a lot more normal. Releasing ads about Medicare-for-All and showcasing photos of him meeting former president Obama was all in hopes of wooing voters in the center. It didn't work, however: his poll numbers have been relatively flat and the financial support engendered has been from his core base of supporters.

This is a useful instruction to any anti-establishment outsider candidate of the future. What gets you to the stage is the message you should stick with. Yang's relentless optimism is what got his gang of supporters together in the first place, and the so-called craziness of what he's saying doesn't sound all that crazy to a lot of people. The more he can force establishment and bigger polling politicians to debate him on *his terms*, the more potential voters that he's likely to gain. He's certainly at a turning point: the question now is what direction that he will choose.

Why Millenial Pete Fell Flat With Millenials

Krystal Ball

Mayor Pete is gay and that's great. I still don't want him to be President. Mayor Pete is a millennial and so am I. That doesn't make me want to support him any more. Actually, it probably has the inverse effect. We are almost the exact same age, only two months apart, and so I know exactly who this guy is. I've met plenty just like him. We didn't really have them in the town I grew up in, but I certainly met them in college and as a young professional and especially at various "convenings" of "young leaders."

In fact, although they may share a similar age bracket, young people who came of age during the financial crisis and the endless wars and destruction of the middle class want nothing to do with Pete's status quo politics. They really don't care whether he's gay or young or Midwestern. They care that he represents more of the same and that's why a November Quinnipiac poll had him at a mere 2% among voters under 35. It's also worth noting that a November poll of LGBTQ voters by Out Magazine and You-Gove found Pete at 4th place among the LGBTQ community as well.[7] As you all know, I love diving into the polling crosstabs and in doing so I found a remarkable and consistent trend. Pete's own age group and sexual orientation may not have much use for him, but there was one demographic that seemed particularly drawn

---

7   https://www.lgbtqnation.com/2019/11/elizabeth-war-ren-top-candidate-among-lgbtq-people-according-new-polling/

to him: Boomers.

Several weeks after writing the essay below, *the New York Times* noticed Pete's Boomer support (are they secret *Rising* watchers?) and wrote an entire article on it. Up to that point however, there had been a sort of vague assumption that Pete was appealing to young people simply based on the fact that he is himself young. I'm pretty sure there is still an assumption that he outperforms in the LGBTQ community in spite of any data to back it up. Pete was actually hilariously talked about as a threat to Bernie's support among college students. That assumption recalls one made of Bernie Sanders back when he burst on the presidential scene in 2016. *The New York Times* wrote a now obviously absurdly wrong article headlined: "Bernie Sanders's Message Resonates with a Certain Age Group: His Own" about how only old people liked Bernie.[8] Pete's failure to find support in the demographic groups that the media expected and predicted is one more perfect example of how in the end, voters care much more about what you'll do than about your age, gender, race or sexual orientation.

November 7, 2019

The vague optimistic platitudes. The promise of "generational change," which really just means the status quo brought to you by a younger dude. The rapid ascent through the echelons of elite status, providing reassurance that the American meritocracy is functioning just fine and is not, in fact, a rotten, soulless fraud designed to rob the masses of dignity. From his anodyne ads to his fake folksy demeanor, it all strikes a certain chord with a very specific group of voters. It's a sort of dog whistle of bland aspiration—the kind you'd find on a motivational poster at the dentist's office.

You all know what I'm getting at here. Mayor Pete Buttigieg is the Boomer candidate. No offense, by the way, to the many individuals who fall in the Boomer age range but do not fall into the typical Boomer mentality. After all, the Boomers I'm talking about here are the affluent sort. The college-educated MSNBC

---

8   https://www.nytimes.com/2015/05/29/us/politics/bernie-sanders-campaign.html

watching type. Pete's strong Boomer base is not just my guess, although it certainly would be my guess even if I didn't have numbers to back it up. I do have numbers though. And they do back it up.

October and November polls show a clear picture of Mayor Pete's base. Buried in the crosstabs of an early November national Monmouth poll, you'll find that while Pete has garnered a mere five percent of supporters under fifty, a full 12 percent of the over-50-crowd is pining for Pete. Economist/YouGov had the most detailed cross tabs, and they have consistently found that Pete's strongest age support came from those over the age of 45. Quinnipiac? Same deal.

As far as I can tell, this is a demographic appeal that is unique to Pete. Obviously, the young folks love Bernie, and the old folks love Biden, but only Pete can turn up that kind of disproportionate strength right in the boomer zone. So, what is it about the Pete pitch that lands with the 55-to-75-year-old demographic?

Well, to start with, Boomers love the *idea* of appealing to young people; they just don't like the revolutionary change politics that come with actually appealing to young people. They think that the way to win millennials is simply by talking about being a millennial. This, of course, is the Mayor Pete way. Forget about devastating climate change, massive debt loads, poverty wages and living in a sixth-floor walk-up closet with four of your friends. *Bloomberg News* is reporting on a new study that shows how the opioid crisis and decades of endless wars have wreaked havoc on the health of millennials; massive problems requiring systemic change way beyond just beating Trump.

Bloomberg News
November 6, 2019
   Headline: Spiking Health Problems in U.S. Millenials May Make Them Poorer
By Emma Court

But none of this seems to register for the affluent Boomer who believes that if we just bring in a young person to say the same old crap, then the young people will love it! I guarantee you that if you asked Pete's supporters where he gets most of his support, they would tell you that it's from those under 30. I see this all the time in the media world. Someone in management will create a new show or product designed to appeal to Millennials, and they go about it by giving people titles like "millennial correspondent." Those projects always get funding, yet never get views.

Let me ask you this, Boomer. Do you like the idea of everyone getting health care coverage, as long as it doesn't cost you anything, and you still get to be at the front of the line? Pete's your guy with Medicare for those who want it! Do you like the feeling of doing something about climate without having to actually change your day to day life or reorient your consumerist values? Pete is there to reassure you on his website that: "as big as this crisis is, our ideas and aspirations are big enough to meet it." Do you believe that our biggest problem is our lack of civility, but also spend countless hours a day watching strangers yell at each other on cable news? Then Mayor Pete, who loves to talk about the things that unite us (except when he's laying into Elizabeth Warren or Beto O'Rourke), is the candidate for you.

You see, for Boomer elites, admitting that there are actually real problems within our system means admitting that they screwed stuff up. They're all about "change," as long as it doesn't mean anything will actually change for them. They're all the way in for a good hopeful optimism that says "*sure, things aren't perfect, but I'm a McKinsey consultant and a Rhodes scholar, and our dreams are as big as our aspirations, which can be achieved if we just work together towards greater goodness of our unified perfection,*" etc, etc, etc.

Plus, he's gay, so just electing him counts as progress, right? Ummm, yeah. OK, Boomer.

Communities Of Color Reject Identity Tokenism

Krystal Ball

When Julián Castro dropped out of the race, another round of existential angst gripped neoliberals as they grappled with the failure to launch of so many candidates of color. The establishment types who mouthed words like "center black women" were gob-smacked that women of color had chosen by and large to back Joe Biden and Bernie Sanders. A rush of tortured explanations and psychoanalysis was offered to explain this perplexing fact. None bothered to consider that maybe if you really wanted to center black women, you would speak directly to the depressed wages and rampant inequality that have disproportionately harmed women of color. Maybe you'd be willing to upend the system that has robbed so many of their basic dignity. They could not wrap their heads around the fact that the vision and approach of a candidate were more relevant to their lives than the candidate's personal background.

I always want to be clear, there are real forces of racism and sexism and they are deeply important. But when you throw around those words casually, they come to mean nothing. When you insinuate that every voter in the country is racist, you lose all credibility. And most importantly, people are no longer willing to believe that just changing the race or the gender of the people in charge is enough.

There's another follow-on effect that I think these folks may not really be thinking about. When Hillary Clinton's 2016 loss was blamed on sexism, what message do you think it sent to every young woman out there thinking of running for office? When Kamala's loss in spite of every advantage is blamed on her race, what message do you think it sends to young black women about their chances in the American political system? It's far too easy and obscures way too much to just pin these failures on identity when there was sooooo much more going on. And by taking the nuance out of it you discourage the very people that you claim to want to champion.

For me personally, all things being equal I will pick a minority or female candidate over a white male candidate. But what does that even mean? It's not like these candidates come out of a factory assembly line identically made and then stamped with a particular identity. Of course they are each unique and bring different strengths and weaknesses to the table, including the experience of their upbringing and background. As they come, I choose just to evaluate each through the lens of who will fight hardest and do the most to make life better for the working class. Whose record and background makes them most likely to do so. That may be an unusual approach for a media figure, but I suspect it lines up pretty closely with how most voters go about making their choice.

January 3, 2020

The news of Julián Castro's departure from the presidential race triggered another avalanche of one of the most bizarre rituals of the 2020 Democratic primary—people pretending to grieve when a candidate they never supported drops out of the race. Twitter had never even heard of Julián Castro until he announced, he could no longer sustain his campaign, and now, all of a sudden, waves of mostly white people are pretending to be despondent and outraged at the loss. The target of their ire? The other white people who supposedly doomed the campaigns of all the candidates of color. Here's a good example of this style of remorse from a Twitter user:

> "I'm upset about Castro. I'm still heartbroken about Kamala. I'm trying not to cry white woman tears about it. But wow did we f*** this up."

Who, by the way, is the "we" in this tweet? Is it just the white women who f'ed things up, or the 99 percent of Democratic primary voters, to include many people of color, who were not supporting Castro? Not to miss out on the pile on, Eugene Robinson penned an op-ed for *The Washington Post* headlined: "Democrats are Starting to Look like a Whites Only Party."

Honestly I actually liked Castro more than many of the other candidates. His time at the United States Department of Housing and Urban Development was bad, but he pushed the field to the left on immigration, he wasn't afraid to talk about poverty, and he took risks. I respect him for it. But please don't give me this nonsense about how his campaign failed because of his race. It doesn't hold up to even a split second of scrutiny.

First of all, the reason that Biden and Bernie are the top two candidates right now isn't, for the most part, because of white people. Their success and durability is precisely because they are disproportionately backed by people of color. Their coalitions are by far the most diverse of any candidate. If you are angry about the failure of people of color in this primary, I guess you should be angry at the voters of color who didn't back them, although I think that would be rather ridiculous and even offensive.

Second, one rationale I've heard for the fact that minority voters are backing Bernie and Joe is that black voters, in particular, are just backing the candidates that they think white voters will like. Here's that take from @emarvelous on Twitter, echoed by many:

> "Gonna keep saying this: Black voters are pragmatic. For many, electability means who white voters are most comfortable with."

This kind of psychoanalysis is just tortured and bizarre. The reason Bernie and Biden are leading isn't complicated. They have the highest favorability ratings. They are most trusted on the issues voters care about. They represent two clear ideological poles of the party and have attracted voters who respond to those distinct visions. It's frankly patronizing to ascribe a motive to voters that they have never articulated. It also ignores the tiny inconvenient fact that Barack Obama both won the Democratic nomination and became President of the United States. Please ask a young black Sanders supporter if they are really just supporting Bernie because they believe old white people will like him and tell me what response you get back. Pretty much every white person I see talking on T.V. seems to hate Sanders' guts and believe that he is not "electable," so I'm not sure how you would come to that conclusion in the first place.

Third, I also saw it argued that the media was biased against Castro because of his identity. You certainly aren't going to find me defending the media. But how, then, do you explain the durability and relative success of candidates of color Andrew Yang and Tulsi Gabbard, who have received harsher and more unfair coverage than Julián, and certainly far worse coverage than one-time media darlings Kamala Harris and Cory Booker? Also, it's not like the media has exactly rolled out the red carpet for Bernie Sanders. Just consider, a writer for Politico magazine found a way to argue that Sanders' massive working-class-driven fundraising haul was really a sign of his support among wealthy white people. I mean seriously people, you can't make this up!

> @billscher: "Your periodic reminder that the small donor class is disproportionately white, wealthy, college educated, and much much smaller than the overall primary electorate"

And yet in spite of their hatred and bias, at the end of the day, it was Bernie who has disproportionately earned the Hispanic support that Castro was banking on.

Julián Castro made a bet with his campaign that as a fairly young Latino, the rising Latino electorate would back him. He's got a good establishment resume. He's got a good personal story. He clearly thought that being the Texan with the immigration focus would pay dividends. But it didn't. Instead, Hispanic voters have responded most strongly to old white guy Bernie Sanders. Why? Well, you should probably ask them first, rather than inventing some kind of weird internalized 'racism' explanation.

I would point out though that the latest Economist/YouGov poll shows the economy, health care, and immigration to be tied for first in issue concerns among Hispanic voters. I know it sounds crazy, so hear me out on this, but maybe—just maybe—Hispanics are supporting Bernie because of his clear stances on those issues, and because he has invested more resources in organizing and communicating authentically within the community than any other campaign. Perhaps they cared more about what he would do for the community than whether or not he happened to be from the community.

The massive stakes involved in choosing a president have been made even more clear by the act of war that President Trump just committed against Iran. Hundreds of thousands of lives now hang in the balance. We're not choosing who we want on a magazine cover or as some sort of promotional branding exercise. We're choosing a president—a commander in chief. What that person will do, the courage they have demonstrated, the principles they bring with them, are endlessly more important than their race, gender, religion, eye color or anything else.

At the end of the day, the folks who are pretending to be bereft at Julián's departure don't even actually care about diversity. If they did, they would celebrate Tulsi and they would celebrate Yang and maybe they would even find the idea of the first Jewish president, a son of immigrants, whose family members were killed in the Holocaust, to be an exciting prospect, especially at a time of rising antisemitism. But no, because the truth is, they only care about diversity when it checks the right ideological boxes. And honestly, there's nothing wrong with that. You support a candidate because of what they stand for. No problem. But don't dress it up as something else. Don't act like it makes you morally superior because you pretended to be saddest at Kamala and Julián's departures. How about you give everyone else the right to support the candidates who match their ideology as well? Even if that means supporting an old white guy.

IV.
THEORIES
OF CHANGE

Theories of Change

This is where the rubber hits the road. Where the theoretical becomes reality. How in an era of "gridlock" do you not just cobble together the necessary coalition to win but actually make the sweeping changes that will transform the country? How do you make the sort of changes of an FDR or an LBJ or a Reagan? How do you force a political realignment that sets the stage for decades to come? This is maybe the most consequential question we attempt to address. Because it's all well and good to offer plans and ideas and soaring rhetoric, but what does it all amount to? Can you shift the Overton window of what's possible? Can you win? Can you implement your ideas?

We know what hasn't worked. We know that begging the opposition party to help you absent public pressure isn't going to get the job done. We know that transformational change won't spring instantaneously from one leader, whether that be Barack Obama counting on his personal brilliance or Donald Trump banking on his ability to charm and negotiate. In fact, both the Obama and Trump administrations are filled with cautionary tales and learnings that any would-be-political-revolutionary should heed.

Barack Obama swept into office with an incredible grassroots movement. His campaign was a pioneer in small-dollar fundraising and online organizing. An entire generation was caught up in the excitement and gave money for the first time, volunteered for the first time, *believed* for the first time. As this grassroots movement was organizing itself in neighborhoods and on social media, a coalition of Wall Street and Silicon Valley donors was also coalescing around the young political phenom, who was raising a record-breaking amount of money from the financial sector.

After Obama won and was inaugurated, rather than relying on and empowering the grassroots movement, he instead turned to Wall Street. Under the leadership of Chief of Staff Rahm Emanuel—who had himself cashed in over a number of years on Wall Street—Obama's administration was staffed up with finance-friendly types like Timothy Geithner and former Clinton Treasury Secretary Larry Summers. His massive grassroots organizing operation was more or less dismantled. The message was: "Thank you very much, I've got it from here." Rather than rallying the public to pressure lawmakers to pass his initiatives, he placed his faith in his own ability to lecture and cajole them into doing what he wanted. Unsurprisingly, it didn't work very well, even though he took office with control of the House, a supermajority in the Senate, and a crisis that more than justified transformative action. Rather than fall back on the waves of idealistic young people and African Americans who carried him to office, he more often stabbed them in the back. He refused to demand a public option in healthcare. He repeatedly went to Republicans in search of a Social Security-cutting grand bargain. He failed to help the disproportionately minority homeowners who were losing everything thanks to his Wall Street friends.

With this approach, it should be no surprise that under his watch, Democrats fell out of favor in most of the country. They lost nearly 1,000 state legislative seats, were tossed out of Governor's mansions, lost the House and then the Senate, ultimately ushering in the era of Donald Trump. History is likely to look back at the Obama years as an unbelievable missed opportunity. He had it well within his power to reorient the Democratic Party around the working class, but instead he continued to move it towards the wealthy and the upper middle class. It remains to be seen whether the tide can be turned back.

In his way, Donald Trump has made many of the same mistakes that Obama did. He too was brought to power by the combination of a passionate grassroots movement and a wealthy donor class. As we write this, while risking another potential Middle Eastern war that would enrich defense contractors and devastate the American working class, it could not be more clear who's counsel he has heeded since taking office. Like Obama, he staffed up with Wall Street types like Gary Cohn, Steve Mnuchin and Stephen Schwarzman. Absurdly, he began his administration with establishment ghouls like Reince Priebus and Sean Spicer in key positions. He has continued holding campaign rallies with his die-hard supporters but he has yet to deliver on some key administration priorities. He has never used the considerable data operation at his fingertips to organize around key campaign promises like immigration, instead relying on a largely cartoonishly incompetent staff that could not even manage to get a question on the census changed.

In the Democratic primary, one candidate really stands out for their commitment to a different theory of change. Bernie Sanders is well known for his policy positions on Medicare-for-All and the $15 minimum wage, but if you had to identify the core of his campaign, it's really his commitment to what he calls a "political revolution." When asked how he'll get things done in office, he doesn't talk about negotiating with the other side or legislative tactics, he talks about serving as Organizer in Chief, rallying the public to his side, and forcing intransigent lawmakers to get on board or risk the wrath of the electorate. In Rules for Radicals, Saul Alinsky writes that: "Action comes from keeping the heat on. No politician can sit on a hot issue if you make it hot enough." That is very much Sanders' belief and the argument that he makes.

This approach, more than anything else, is what differentiates Sanders from the other candidates in the Democratic primary. It's the core reason why his coalition looks so different from fellow progressive Elizabeth Warren. Her disproportionately affluent supporters find her technocratic approach more comfortable. They have faith in experts. They are the experts. They believe in legislating as a negotiation between bureaucratic elites where the President's own intellect is the primary driving force. Sometimes Warren is compared to Hillary Clinton and it's true, they both love a good white paper, but perhaps the more apt comparison is to Obama and his abiding faith in his own powerful intellect.

Before having the chance to put his political revolution into action however, Sanders first has to get elected and there are clearly major obstacles in his path. Biden's electability and restoration argument has a firm and enduring foothold in the Democratic primary, especially among older voters. But there would be major obstacles in a potential general election as well. Sanders' electability and efficacy in office rests on his ability to stitch together a multi-racial working class coalition. That is the ultimate goal and endgame of his campaign. But as Saagar points out, the fixation on identity and woke cultural signaling that is ascendant on the left, may render Sanders' movement unacceptable to the more culturally conservative and nationalistic portions of the white working class. This cultural mismatch has been a stumbling block for leftist movements in the UK and elsewhere.

In this chapter, we examine what tactics and movements have worked and what has failed, both here and overseas. We warn the right about thinking you can win by just yelling "socialism sucks." We warn the left about pandering to identities while selling the whole working class out to corporate interests. We look to the past for clues on how any anti-establishment administration might be able to overcome the immense opposition they will face once in office.

There may truly be no more important topic in American politics. The fashionable cynical view of Washington is that it's all gridlock. That nothing can get done. That it may well be impossible to try. We fully admit that on the one hand, the obstacles are daunting. On the other hand, Trump's real legacy will be how he exposed the hollowness and fragility of every major American institution. He's run roughshod over their cherished "norms and guardrails" and nothing and no one has been able to stop him. What would happen if the public was actually enlisted in the service of a pro-working class agenda? What might Obama have accomplished if he hadn't disbanded his movement? What might Trump have done if he had been able to staff his administration with like-minded people and galvanized his adoring fans into action rather than simply asking them to put all their faith in him? What might Democrats have been able to extract from this administration if they had put a quarter of the energy they spent on Russia and Ukraine into fighting for an increased minimum wage or health care or union rights? Maybe the pundits are right, maybe better things really aren't possible. But our radical history and the unsustainable rot of the status quo say otherwise.

In Kentucky it was Socialism and Class Warfare For the Win!

Krystal Ball

National Democrats were extremely excited after winning the Governor's mansion back in Kentucky. "See look" they proclaimed, impeachment is helping us or at least not hurting! In fact this is precisely the wrong conclusion to draw. The way that Kentucky Democrats won this race stands in complete opposition to the approach and daily obsessions of the national Democratic establishment.

Kentucky Dems didn't waste their time obsessing over Bevin's violations of "norms and guardrails" and they certainly didn't spin out wild foreign conspiracy theories even though there was fodder for some. In particular, a Russian-backed aluminum plant broke ground in Eastern Kentucky with help from Bevin and McConnell. This development garnered news coverage of course, but was far from the center of Democratic candidate Andy Beshear's critique.

They also didn't spend their days attacking Bevin's supporters as racist or sexist or stupid or condescendingly chastise them for "voting against their interests." Instead, they relentlessly focused on three core economic issues: healthcare, education, and union rights. They leveraged the energy of a massive teacher's movement in the state and ran a campaign hyper-focused on issues that actually impact people's day to day lives. Meanwhile, Bevin was the one clinging to Washington for dear life, playing up his Trump relationship at every chance and ob-

sessively talking about impeachment. In the end, it was extremely close, but Kentucky voters chose working class politics over DC
parlor games. National Democrats should learn from this. I'm
not holding my breath.

November 6, 2019

Democrats have won back the governor's mansion in
Kentucky—a state Donald Trump won by 30 points in 2016. They
did it by driving up the margins in the urban and suburban areas,
but also by outperforming in a Donald Trump stronghold—the
coal counties in the eastern part of the state.

If you aren't a Kentuckyphile like me, here were the basic dynamics of the race: Kentucky has long been Democratic
at the state level, but that trend had completely reversed in the
Trump era. In fact, the just-defeated Republican governor, Matt
Bevin—a brash outsider businessman—was ushered into office
in 2015 on a populist wave that, in many ways, foreshadowed
Trump's national victory.

Bevin proceeded to govern as the jerkiest member of the
Chamber of Commerce, promptly implementing union-busting
right-to-work legislation, and fighting tooth-and-nail to strip
Kentuckians of the healthcare that they gained through the Affordable Care Act (ACA) Medicaid expansion, which was more
successfully implemented in Kentucky than in any other state
in the country. The uninsured rate in the state for low-income
adults had dropped from 43 percent to 13. But Bevin really, really
screwed up when he messed with teacher's pensions.

In a lot of rural towns in Kentucky, the school system
is the heartbeat of the community, not to mention one of their
major employers. Not only did Matt Bevin attempt to mess with
their pensions, but insulted the teachers who shut down schools
and rallied at the capitol building in solidarity. He called them
ignorant and thugs, and went so far as to essentially accuse them
of being accessories to sexual assault. In other words, rather than
the outsider populist he ran as, he turned out to be a rich guy
prick who delighted in insulting workers and messing with their
healthcare, unions, and pensions.

I must be honest, the Democratic candidate , Kentucky Attorney General Andy Beshear, is not a phenom in the charisma department. But he does have a well-known last name in the state. His dad was a popular governor who implemented the Medicaid expansion, and from everything I could tell, he ran quite an excellent and disciplined campaign on the ground. This race, though, wasn't about Andy Beshear. It was all about saying 'F-you' to Bevin.

Beshear won by running up the margins in the suburbs and urban areas, but there aren't enough of those in Kentucky to get you over the finish line on their own. It was actually coal country that came through and gave Beshear the numbers he needed to pull off the stunning upset. The eastern part of the state is culturally conservative, yes, but is also economically populist, and they were not having it with Bevin's attacks on workers.

Democrats are rightfully giddy about this result, especially since Don Jr., Pence, and Trump all turned up in the state to try to drag Bevin across the finish line. But, let's be clear: Beshear won *in spite of* national Democrats, not because of them. The populist critique of Bevin is not remotely what Democrats have used to go after Trump.

For example, Kentucky Democrats did not win by launching esoteric attacks on Bevin about the 'norms and guardrails of democracy' or lofty ideals like 'freedom of the press,' even though Bevin is probably even more hostile to the press than Trump. I can promise you that Ukraine, Russia, and impeachment were only ever mentioned by the Republican side. Instead, Democrats pulled off this win by staying lightning-focused on the way that Bevin hurt working-class families.

For me, traveling back to the state was a big reminder about how non-DC and New York elites talk about politics. When I spoke with Teamsters Local 783 president John Stovall, he described Trump in terms that were much more direct and effective than what you often hear from Washington.

"What he's done is he's hurt the middle class and lower-income, and his tax credits and all that have benefited the rich. It hasn't benefited the poor."

Simple. Straightforward. Connected to people's lives. Not contempt-filled or condescending. This kind of messaging is much more effective than the Ukraine/Russia/norms and guardrails hand wringing that you are hit over the head with by the media and Democratic elite.

On the other side, Bevin very much tried to use the dumb "socialism sucks" argument that the Democratic establishment keeps telling us to be terrified of. He tried to tie Andy Beshear to AOC and the Green New Deal and Bernie Sanders. Obviously, it failed. On the day Sanders came to Kentucky for a campaign rally, Bevin posted the following challenge to Kentucky voters on his Twitter account:

> "Bernie Sanders is in Louisville, supporting his friend, Andy Beshear, and spreading his hateful class warfare and communist ideology... Kentucky voters....which side are you on? Do you support socialism or do you still believe that America is the greatest nation on earth?"

Well, I guess it was socialism and class warfare for the win, then! Recent polling of Wisconsin, Pennsylvania, and Michigan have shown that Trump is in a position to win the Electoral College again. This, in spite of the fact that the only story the mainstream media writes is that Trump is bad. Democrats should not use this Kentucky victory as an excuse to feel like everything is going fine with their impeachment strategy and national messaging. Instead, they should use it as an opportunity to learn from this "red state" that unexpectedly turned blue on the back of a working-class populist backlash. Here's my advice. Move on from Ukraine as fast as you possibly can, and embrace the class war.

My Dire Warning
For The American Right

Saagar Enjeti

Donald Trump won the White House by signaling a rejection to free-market orthodoxy. Yet if you visit Washington today, the think tanks and professional Republican class continue to operate as if he ran and won because he promised people a tax cut and never spoke once about immigration or trade.

That's because Washington subsists solely on the beneficence of Wall Street billionaires and others with a direct financial interest in maintaining a status quo economy that does not work for all Americans. Free market libertarianism is a cancer that has firmly intertwined itself with corporatism and is embedded firmly within both parties.

As the conservative host of *Rising* my interest, of course, is in shedding the right of these free-market libertarian forces, by highlighting just how stupid it sounds to the youth and working class of this country when you tell them that the economy has never been better for humans before in history.

This essay was inspired after finding out that the head of the Congressional committee responsible for regulating banks actually threw a birthday party for financial giant AIG in their committee room. That party occurred on almost the exact same date where a poll revealed that millennials overwhelmingly accept socialism, something I am vehemently opposed to.

I believe we are condemned to a socialist future if the American right does not shed the oligarchical and corporate forces within it and orient all its policies, even if that means government action, towards the singular goal of more equitable wealth and the ability for Americans to live their lives as they want in a place of their choosing. Some on the right have expanded on this, with Senator Marco Rubio, for example, laying out a vision in a National Review op-ed for "common-good capitalism," which understands that "workers have a right to share in the benefits of the profits they helped create" and that "dignified work, strong families, and strong communities are key to civic — and economic — well-being." Republicans should become more comfortable with using the power of the government to help direct market forces toward the goal of conserving our American way of life, American workers, and American families. It is the only viable path forward.

October 30, 2019

I spend a lot of time talking about the 2020 Democratic Election. But every once in awhile, we need to turn an eye toward our decrepit city in Washington to highlight just how exactly we got to a point where polling indicates that almost half the American public wants to burn our institutions to the ground. Just recently was a prime example, something that our elites didn't even try to hide: the House Ways and Means Committee threw a bipartisan birthday party for insurance company AIG, which was widely attended by staffers across the aisle. Richard Neal, the chairman of the committee and a Democrat, gave remarks at the party. It included snacks and an open bar serving a "centennial smash" signature cocktail. An a cappella group serenaded the attendees to the tune of Pharell's 'Happy'.

This is Versailles-1790s-level decadence, and it is a repulsive illustration of the bipartisan corruption that has seeped into our system. Don't forget, AIG is the company that received 190 billion dollars in bailout funds a decade ago, while the rest of the American middle class plummeted to destruction. It's also the same company that paid out 165 million dollars in bonuses to its executives after receiving bailout money and faced absolutely zero repercussions from the Obama administration.

Yet that same company which was saved by the United States government was thrown a birthday party in the halls of the United States Congress? It literally doesn't get more corrupt than that. These people are so shameless: they bragged about this party and they allowed it to be reported in *Politico* because that's just business as usual in our capital city.

Corporatism knows no political party. It has wormed its way into the highest levels of the United States government and has ruled us to our detriment for almost 40 years now. The left has responded to this moment with Democratic Socialism. The right looking at this movement is learning all the wrong lessons. They're flying 'Socialism Sucks' banners all across America without acknowledging the underlying structure of the American system as extraordinarily flawed.

So many on the right label the Millennial generation and the working class as *lazy*, and give no credence to why exactly we're angry. We watched our money get sent to Wall Street while our student debt exploded and any surplus cash was spent trying to turn the Middle East into a democratic paradise. America voted twice for change agent Barack Obama to try and clean up the system, but he mostly just lectured corporations with an upturned chin and wagging finger while abetting their continued shipment of American jobs to China and Mexico.

Institutionalized corruption has yielded disastrous results. A new survey from the *Victims of Communism Memorial Foundation* finds that more than 70 percent of millennials say they are likely to vote Socialist and that 1-in-5 think that America would be better off if private property was abolished. This makes perfect sense to me, because this generation sees the AIG bailout and the party on Capitol Hill 10 years later, and thinks: "Well, if that's capitalism, then this crap is not for me."

I know some of the people reading this probably are actual socialists. But maybe you're just fed up and you've been told that if you're against our current system, then you must be a socialist. So you shrug and go: "Sure, I guess." It is incumbent upon the American Right to restore an equitable and fair playing field within our system if we, correctly in my view, believe that capitalism is intrinsic to the strength of the United States.

That being said, the libertarian streak of the Republican Party will be the electoral and moral death of it. Libertarianism was founded upon the idea that the greatest threat to you and your life is institutionalized power in the form of the government. It's time they understood that the government isn't the only institution that can hold power in our society.

How Theories of Change Separate Bernie from Warren

Krystal Ball

Fairly early in the 2020 cycle, Saagar and I noted something that most political observers did not catch onto until far later, if at all. In spite of the fact that both Warren and Bernie occupied the same "progressive" quadrant in the minds of the commentariat, they held vastly different appeal to very different groups of voters. Warren's coalition was whiter and more affluent. Bernie's was more diverse and more working class. In other words, Warren was a wine track candidate and Bernie was a beer track candidate.

The media of course loved to claim that the two candidates were really exactly the same. Now partly, this was more self-serving analysis, since Warren with her affluent white appeal is a media favorite. If Bernie and Warren are really the same in all other ways, why wouldn't you pick the woman who was also a bit younger? Partly, it reflected a failure to understand the way voters select candidates, which is often more cultural and less ideological. For example, despite occupying very different places on the ideological spectrum, Bernie and Biden actually tend to have more coalition overlap than Bernie and Warren. And partly, it's because their surface-level, identity-focused analysis is completely oblivious to theories of change and that is where the key differences between Sanders and Warren really lie.

In August, I knew of course how I thought about the differences between Sanders and Warren, but I wanted to hear directly from supporters of each about how they thought about it. I took the question to Twitter. The response was overwhelming and ultimately very edifying. Sanders supporters had already keyed in on Warren's wishy-washy support of Medicare-for-All, even while at the time she was still insisting "I'm with Bernie" on healthcare. They were skeptical of her commitment to movement politics, even before her comment that "I'm just a player in the game." I received far fewer responses from Warren supporters, in itself a sign that her coalition is quite different from Bernie's. Her supporters, though, appreciated that her approach was more incremental. They believed her to be more detailed and thorough, and Bernie to be more of a big picture thinker than an effective implementer.

In many ways, the essay below set up a lot of how I thought about Bernie, Warren and the other 2020 Democratic candidates as well. Digging into these coalitions and different theories of change allowed us to predict accurately that Warren would benefit from Kamala's fall and be hurt by Pete's rise. It helped us to understand the durability of both Biden and Bernie even as others constantly predicted their demise. Maybe Twitter is good for something after all.

August 19, 2019

So, I may have opened a whole can of worms recently. Let me explain. There is new data out from Pew Research confirming that, contrary to conventional media wisdom, Elizabeth Warren and Bernie Sanders appeal to strikingly different coalitions. In particular, of all the candidates, Warren's prime constituency is the most highly educated and the most white. Bernie's is the least likely to be college-educated and the least white. (R.I.P. to the 'Bernie Bros' narrative.)

Pew Research Center
August 16, 2019
Headline: Most Democrats Are Excited by 'Several' 2020 Candidates - Not Just Their Top Choice
Electability Matters to Democrats but so do policies, character

These different coalitions fit with other polling we've seen, and also fit with the fact that Warren and Sanders have seemed to rise in the polls simultaneously post-debate, so they are not cannibalizing each other's supporters. I have my theories about why all of this is, but shockingly just because I think it doesn't always make it correct. So, I did what one does: I asked Twitter. I asked people who had strong feelings for Warren and against Bernie, or for Bernie and against Warren, to explain why — and boy did they. Nearly 3,000 people chimed in about how they felt, and it was fascinating and surprisingly substantive, considering, you know, it was Twitter. I want you all to know that I read all of what was posted through yesterday evening. There were some really interesting common themes. The idea, for example, that Bernie had been more consistent and showed up for fights that Warren did not. One user, @WinkleBerns, wrote: "Unlike most other Dems, I don't hate Warren. But you put her track record up against Bernie and there's no contest. He's been advocating on the same issues and policies his whole life. Liz was a Republican until the 90s. The 2016 primary and Standing Rock revealed her."

Standing Rock and Warren's politically calculated Clinton endorsement in 2016 came up a lot, as did her tepid support of Medicare-for-All. But if you boiled a lot of the conversation down, it came down to theories of political change. Those of you who watch the show regularly know that for me, this is the most important issue as well.

Here's a pro-Bernie framing from @IramiOF that I really thought cut right to the heart of the matter: "Labor. Warren wants to redistribute through top down bureaucracy. Sanders wants to democratize political power. That's the difference between Sanders' economic bill of rights and Warrens (sic) 'economic patriotism.'" By the way, you can find Irami on YouTube as "The Funky Academic."

Warren supporters, too, talked a lot about theories of change. They described Warren as more pragmatic or more realistic. I thought this take by @allenredux was quite interesting: "He [Bernie] loses me and my progressive friends when he says things like felons in prison should vote. How about we concentrate on voter suppression etc first. Warren is more practical choice for me."

And @allenredux is absolutely right that fighting for incarcerated persons to vote is not "pragmatic" in any sense of the word. There is no pollster who would tell you to take this position. No panel of Midwestern moms who would back letting murderers or drug dealers vote. But, for Sanders supporters, that's kind of the point. If you are committed to democratizing political power, then fighting for voting rights for all citizens, even those who are incarcerated, is an important, even vital fight. Think about this: if you can disenfranchise any group of people you don't like simply by trapping them in our mass incarceration system, then you can do anything you want. And make no mistake, that is, in fact, a core part of why so many black and brown and poor men are criminalized. But it's even worse than just having your political power stripped away. Federal prisons are often located in rural red-state America. Those held are counted by the census for purposes of apportioning political power even as they are denied the ability to exercise that power. So their bodies are literally being used to empower Republican politicians with whom they often profoundly disagree and who have profoundly harmed them.

This is a key difference between Sanders and Warren. One candidate looks at voting for incarcerated persons and says I don't see a lever that exists for me to pull to make this happen; the other says we will build the damn lever. This really may be the most important dividing line for Democratic primary contenders. Warren, Biden, Buttigieg, Harris—they have some different policy ideas but they are all planning to play the game as it exists. Out of the folks that I just named there is zero doubt in my mind that Warren would play the game the best. She's brilliant. She knows what to do. She's experienced in working the levers of government. But what if that's not enough? Not enough to combat a climate crisis, and a white nationalist crisis, and an automation crisis. What if the idea of working together for change with Mitch McConnell is more of an unworkable fantasy than democratizing power through a political revolution? Bernie's theory of change may not be "practical," but it may be the best shot we've got.

Can a 'Player In The Game' Also Be a Revolutionary?

Krystal Ball

Sometimes a candidate's greatest strength is also their greatest weakness. That has turned out to be the case for Massachusetts Senator Elizabeth Warren. She rose with voters and in the esteem of the media by getting the right answer on progressive issues but also promising to be a team player for the Democratic establishment. By railing against a rigged system in one breath and assuring everyone for whom those comments are too edgy that she's a "capitalist to her bones." Squaring those circles worked until it didn't.

If there's one thing I've learned in politics it's that the supposedly "safe" approach almost never is. Ask Hillary Clinton or Jeb Bush. If you aren't willing to lead clearly with the courage of your convictions, why would anyone follow you? It's one of the key mistakes that we saw made over and over again in this race. Candidates like Kamala and Warren get caught up on where the "right" place to be is on an issue, based on the polling or the donor feedback, and they lose sight of the fact that what voters want most is to see your courage, your tenacity, that you're not going to break down the minute the going gets tough.

In comments to Amy Goodman of *Democracy Now!*, Warren accidentally showed the core brittleness of her campaign and a central irreconcilable tension. You can't straddle the line between establishment and anti-establishment. You're either in or you're out. Warren's attempt to have it both ways and her ac-

201

knowledgement to Goodman that in truth she was "just a player in the game" was perhaps the most revealing comment of her primary campaign. This was a key moment when the difference between Warren and Sanders became clear and undeniable.

November 11, 2019

Throughout this campaign, Elizabeth Warren has cultivated an image of being relentlessly cheerful and unflappable. Never cross. Always ready with a plan or a folksy quip or a tale from her upbringing on the ragged edge of the middle class. A sort of peppy silver sneakers cheerleader with the right answer always ready to go. But every once in a while, her mask slips, and always during circumstances where she is caught off guard.

The problem is, she hasn't faced much in terms of tough questioning. Unlike Sanders, Buttigieg, Tulsi, and others, she refuses to go on FOX News and is generally very careful about the interviews she sits for. So you end up with things like this CNN interview with her husband which was so extraordinarily fluffy that Saagar did a whole monologue on it. The toughest question was to her husband, Bruce Mann: "If she does become the nominee, she will go up against President Trump. Are you ready for that?"

Warren also gave an interview to Entertainment Weekly on her favorite T.V. show, which is allegedly *Ballers* on HBO, starring Dwayne 'The Rock' Johnson. Most of the media is more interested in writing exposés on her selfie lines than on actually challenging her in non-stupid ways. But every once in awhile, she gets hit with a real question. Remember this moment on the campaign trail when right after dropping a seven-figure ad buy focused on anti-corruption, she got asked whether her plan would have barred Hunter Biden from sitting on the board of Burisma?

Reporter: Can you say whether or not, under a Warren administration, would your vice president's child be allowed to serve on the board of a foreign company?

Elizabeth Warren: No. I don't—I don't—I-I don't know. I mean,

I-I'd have to go back and look at the details on the plan.

Reporter: Do you think there could be a problem with that?

Elizabeth Warren: I have to go back and look.

If you watch the clip, you can just see the political calculation in real-time. She wants to say "no" because she knows that Hunter Biden serving on that board during the Obama administration was wrong, but she doesn't want to say "no" because she doesn't want to miss the chance to be Biden's VP or Treasury secretary, or whatever, if he does end up in the White House. There's no way to get the answer "right," and so she sort of panics.

And how can we forget the time when radio host of *The Breakfast Club*, Charlamagne tha God, asked Warren when she knew that she wasn't Native American. Charlamagne pressed her repeatedly, and yet she had no answer. He even called her "the original Rachel Dolezal" and still received no response other than getting her to repeat: "This is what I learned from my family."

No answer to the question that has dogged her most consistently since she entered political life; answering would require an admission of some sort—an admission of dishonesty or potentially unfair benefits or cultural appropriation. There's no way to get the right answer. She can't get an "A" on this one, so she becomes evasive and doesn't actually answer when she first found out the truth about her heritage, just as she dodges the question on Hunter Biden.

Well, there's a new incident to enter into the books, and it wasn't pretty. At the environmental justice presidential forum in South Carolina, the incomparable Amy Goodman asked Warren a very fair and important question about the primary process. Here's the exchange:

Amy Goodman: "Speaking about racial injustice, do you think the order of primary states should change? You have Iowa, and New Hampshire, they—"

Elizabeth Warren: "Wait, let me just—before you finish. Are you actually going to ask me to sit here and criticize Iowa and New Hampshire?"

Amy Goodman: "No, I am asking about the order—"

Elizabeth Warren: "No, that is what Iowa and New Hampshire are all about." [Laughs]

Amy Goodman: "But, but, let me just ask—they're two of the whitest states in the country. And then we move to South Carolina, with a very significant population of people of color, and it means the candidates spend so much of their time catering to those first two states. Overall, do you think that should change?"

Elizabeth Warren: "Look, I'm just a player in the game on this one. And I am delighted to be in South Carolina. Thank you."

'I'm just a player in the game.' This entire interaction was very revealing. First of all, Warren thought this question—which was totally reasonable and fair, especially given the context of the forum—was out of bounds; that it was unreasonable for her to have to answer a question that could put her in politically treacherous waters. She objects straight away. How dare Goodman put her in a tough position! As with questions about her heritage, and her corruption plan vis-à-vis Hunter Biden, this was not in the range of questions that anyone was *supposed* to ask her (because there is no 'safe' political answer). For Warren, if you say "yes, the process is flawed," then you piss off key voters in early states. If you say "no, the process is great," then you risk the wrath of people of color who are subordinated in this process by the fact that two extremely white states get to set the tone for the entire primary. There's no briefing book you can study or expert you can consult, and thus Warren finds herself flummoxed and pissed about it.

But then her answer was even more revealing: "I'm just a player in the game." Honestly, if Warren ever was the nominee, Trump could just run this on a loop in every ad. He could plaster it on billboards, because it is so unintentionally honest and damningly so. It strikes to the core of the problem with Warren's campaign. It encapsulates what makes her feel so inauthentic. She's an insider through-and-through—*just a player in the game*—masquerading as a revolutionary, co-opting the language of movements, and talking about big structural change. She's play-acting the part of the class warrior. And while there are good things to be said about effective players in the game, the public has made clear that they are done with *all* the players of the game. Because if you're playing the existing game, the working class always loses. As a friend of mine, Irami (@IramiOF), put it on Twitter: "This is the person that's going to lead large structural change?"

In the grand scheme of things, answering a question about Iowa and New Hampshire is nothing, yet it requires the smallest modicum of political courage just to answer what she so obviously thinks but does not want to say—that, yes, the primary process is less than ideal. But Warren can't get a "B" on the test, she has to get an "A." As a natural pleaser, an "A" student, and a rule-follower myself, I get it. I really do. But it is such a massive and easily exploited weakness.

First of all, if she were to ever become president, the only questions that come to you are of the unsafe, no-win type. But also, when you have to get an "A," it makes it easy for people to screw with you. Trust me, I've seen it. I've lived it. That *need* to get an "A" is why she did this whole catastrophically stupid DNA test to avoid admitting that she had screwed up by claiming native heritage. It's why she went to such elaborate and counterproductive lengths to avoid admitting that middle-class taxes will go up under Medicare-for-All. It's why in 2016 she waited until the outcome was clear and then endorsed Hillary Clinton, and it's why despite all her protests to the contrary, she will never be a revolutionary—always *just a player in the game.*

Bernie Sanders, Cenk Uygur, And The Eventual Downfall of The American Left

Saagar Enjeti

One of the funnier comments I get from people who watch *Rising* is "are you actually conservative?" The answer is yes, I just happen to question free-market orthodoxy. My conservatism is most manifested in my tolerance and support for family values and explicit rejection of intersectionality.

I have openly stated many times that the left's Achilles heel is their total cultural overreach amplified by a woke media that seeks to push identity politics in lieu of class politics. Unfortunately for the working class left of the United States, they have unwittingly tied themselves to the worst woke actors, leaving them exposed for a major rejection in the U.S.

This was best displayed when Bernie Sanders unendorsed Young Turks founder Cenk Uygur for some past uncouth statements dredged up by opposition researchers. Bernie Sanders' decision to bow to the woke Twitter mob reveals to me how he might act as a President of the United States.

While Bernie may be a true class warrior in his heart, he will simply have to bow in incidents like this to the woke identitarian members of his movement. This cultural overreach spells electoral doom for any progressive candidate in the United States, especially in the swing states that were lost to Donald Trump.

This essay was written right after Bernie's un-endorsement of Cenk and aims to critically show the real dangers for the progressive movement in the United States.

December 16, 2019

A remarkable thing happened recently. Senator Bernie Sanders unendorsed Cenk Uygur after "controversial things" he's said resurfaced on Twitter. The timeline of events is a devastating indictment of Sanders and revealed just how much power the intersectionally woke few on Twitter have over the broader American left.

The saga began Thursday when Sanders issued a statement endorsing Uygur for now-resigned Congresswoman Katie Hill's seat in California. Quickly, Twitter mobs began to recirculate Uygur's misogynistic blog posts from nearly 20 years ago, some sexist comments he made on Joe Rogan's show many years ago, and a few other things. What he said was unquestionably bad and there is zero defense of it, as he himself has acknowledged in his apology.

The more and more traction Uygur's past statements got, the more mainstream journalists began to tweet them out, putting immense pressure on the Sanders campaign. How the exact un-endorsement came to be is relatively unclear. Uygur told *The Washington Post* that he spoke with Sanders on Friday and told him he would rather lose his own election than impair the Senator's campaign, before he released a statement saying he would reject *all* endorsements in the race.

The Hill
December 13, 2019
Headline: Sanders revokes congressional endorsement for Young Turks founder Cenk Uygur
By Tal Axelrod

Sanders followed Uygur's announcement with a retraction of his endorsement, making sure to say that his movement is "bigger than one person," a clear distancing move. Now consider this: Bernie Sanders un-endorsed Cenk Uygur, a man who has probably raised millions of dollars for his campaign over the years through the creation of his news network, The Young Turks, but Sanders also still continues to maintain politically toxic Linda Sarsour as a campaign surrogate.

The turnaround on Uygur took all but 24 hours, and the bowing to the outrage mob by the many people involved in this demonstrates who has the real power on the American left, and who exactly can determine what moves for political expediency can be made by these candidates. Anyone with common sense knows that Sanders bowed to the outrage mob because the woke elements of the California Democratic Primary already had their knives out for Uygur, and Bernie desperately wants to win that state as Super Tuesday comes along.

The best part is that most of the people who were "outraged" at Uygur's past statements did not care whatsoever about what he said before he announced his campaign. If any of the people who did Tweet about it want to prove their outrage bonafides, then they can show me their outraged Tweets at homophobic blog posts made by MSNBC host Joy Reid years ago. I won't wait with bated breath for that evidence. The past statements were not made out of genuine concern but as a political weapon against a person who has railed against the mainstream media narrative for many years.

The entire episode validates a core problem for Bernie Sanders, Elizabeth Warren, and other members of the American left. No matter how much you want to tout progressive economics, the intersectionally woke members of your coalition will always impose their PC litmus tests upon you. They will not allow a single concession from these candidates to the cultural right and will demand representation in any future administration they are likely to hold.

If they are rebuffed, then they'll scream like hell and get their media allies to assist them in brutalizing you in the national press. The thing is, if a progressive actually wanted to win in this country, then concessions or at least a degree of respect for the other side is needed on cultural issues. This is the only way that states like Michigan, Pennsylvania, Ohio, Wisconsin, and others will ever get back into the Democratic column.

While the American left is eating its own, my brethren on the Right are beginning to wake up. The Conservative Party in Britain has successfully distanced itself from economic libertarianism with concessions to the left on healthcare, climate change, and the minimum wage. Their economically center-left policies are married to a staunch defense of conservative cultural values. The result is the most successful election in modern UK history for the Conservative Party.

Donald Trump somewhat tapped into this in 2016, and if National Conservatives win the brewing Republican civil war over the future of the Right, then similar returns are guaranteed in our favor. The American left would do well to listen if they want to compete, because the marriage of woke Twitter with progressive economics is doomed to complete failure.

Jeremy Corbyn's Loss Foreshadows Doom For The American Left

Saagar Enjeti

Jeremy Corbyn is not Bernie Sanders. Britain is not America. With those caveats expressed, it is still useful to draw threads between the contemporary American left and its counterpart across the Atlantic Ocean. Corbyn went down in electoral flames in the United Kingdom chiefly because he did not take a strong stance on Brexit. However, the reason he took the Labour Party to its worst defeat in decades lies in his alliance between a progressive economic policy with the intersectional woke left.

Corbyn's alliance came at the exact moment that Boris Johnson's Conservative Party rejected much of its free-market ideology in favor of defending the British state. Johnson's party also made key concessions on healthcare and climate change, allowing it to be a defender of the British economy and most importantly Britain's culture.

This essay is meant to warn the American left that their correct stance on economic issues will be rejected if it is paired with an elite effort to change the cultural fabric of the United States.

December 13, 2019

The British Labour Party saw a resounding defeat in the 2019 UK elections, losing 71 seats in parliament while the Conservatives, led by Boris Johnson, gained a historic 51.

Immediately, American prognosticators began trying to draw parallels between our own elections. Did it mean that Bernie Sanders and Elizabeth Warren-style progressivism are certain to lose handily at the polls? Does it foreshadow a victory for President Trump? Is it even analogous to the U.S. election at all?

The answer is kind of 'yes' to all of the above, with this caveat: the British election was unique in that it came as close to a single-issue election as things can in a modern democracy. Corbyn was very much mealy-mouthed on where he stood on Brexit. But his social message and campaign were built around preserving the British National Health Service (NHS), combined with about as close of an embrace of international democratic socialism as we've seen yet in a Western democratic election. There is no denying, though, that it failed.

The electoral death knell of the progressive left will come from its marriage of correct critiques about our economic system with a wholesale embrace of social justice issues, critical race theory, and de facto open borders via a lack of belief in immigration enforcement. This is especially true in instances where a right-leaning party is able to ditch some of its more libertarian free-market obsessions, like, say, declaring yourself independent from a single European market.

Labour
June 7, 2019
Headline: Labour to put social justice at the heart of everything a Labour government will do with new Social Justice Commission
By Angela Rayner and Jeremy Corbyn

That's exactly what happened in the UK election. Traditional Labour voting areas embraced the Conservative Party message which deviated significantly from the past free-market ideology—rhetoric you might have heard from that same party as recently as 2015. As journalist Zaid Jilani pointed out on Twitter, the "Anglo world left has [the] same problem everywhere, culturally niche, and thinks it can buy off voters with economic policy to make up for that. But if voters don't trust that you respect or even like them they won't pay much attention to the policy promises to begin with."

When you hear me praise Elizabeth Warren's trade policy but say she'll lose because she puts gender pronouns in her Twitter bio, makes fun of people who don't believe in gay marriage, and wants to wear a pink Planned Parenthood scarf on Inauguration Day, this is what I'm talking about. And she's not the only one.

Virtually the entire Democratic field from Joe Biden to Bernie Sanders has committed to a blanket stopping of immigration enforcement in reaction to Donald Trump's election. It cannot be emphasized enough how much of an electoral, let alone economic disaster, that this would entail. A person you may find familiar, Senator Bernie Sanders, once recognized this very fact only 12 years ago, where he said, "If poverty is increasing, and if wages are going down, I don't know why we need millions of people to be coming into this country as guest workers who will work for lower wages than American workers and drive wages down even lower than they are right now."

Bernie has since signed onto an immigration plan which would literally stop immigration enforcement into the U.S., doing exactly what he warned of 12 years ago, except this time the effects of neoliberalism on our economic system are even more pronounced and mass immigration is even more detrimental. Add free healthcare for all these illegal immigrants and you've got yourself an electoral disaster in the making.

Mass immigration, embrace of social justice, and making fun of social conservatism is fundamentally an insult to the many working-class voters that progressive economic policies are designed to help. In each case, they're designed to prioritize somebody else over your own countrymen, designed to disadvantage workers at the expense of whatever group is declared marginalized, and then to demonize the faith that brings light to millions of people.

Corbynism is a dire warning to the American left. Neoliberals from the right and left will tell you it's because of his embrace of the NHS, but the real reason is a total cultural mismatch with everyday people in Britain.

You Can't Poll-Test Your Way To The Presidency

Krystal Ball

Sometimes you just get lucky. On December 2nd I delivered the following monologue wondering whether Kamala was about to drop out of the Presidential race. On the very next day, she dropped out. Well, they don't call me Krystal Ball for nothing! (Ugh, sorry. I of all people should know that the name jokes are terrible!)

The demise of her campaign was easy to see coming. She'd plummeted out of "top tier status," hadn't budged an inch in Iowa since declaring she was moving to the state, and disgruntled staff were starting to throw each other under the bus to every outlet that would listen. At a more fundamental level though, the grave errors and misjudgments in Kamala's campaign were evident even before they were fully realized in the polls. She completely failed to answer for herself or for voters that most basic question of politics: "Why are you running?"

The truth is, Kamala could never properly answer that question because the real answer was both glaringly obvious and damning. Kamala was running for President because Kamala wanted to run for President. The same discredited political establishment types who would encourage Deval Patrick to jump in the race because he's like Mayor Pete only black, so surely he can win over black voters, encouraged Kamala to jump in the race for the same shallow reasons. As an establishment-friendly Democrat with plenty of donor ties and a trail-blazing identity, Kamala ticked a lot of boxes for people who are really all about preserving the status quo. In reality, a change in identity is no substitute for actual change.

The theory went that as a black woman she would steal black voters from Biden and Bernie. With California earlier in the lineup, she'd have a strong home state advantage. As it turned out, voters didn't much care that Kamala was a black woman. They did care quite a lot that she seemed to have no core values or message. This essay is specifically about the failures of the Harris campaign, but the majority of candidates in the race could learn a lot from her mistakes.

December 2, 2019

If you've been watching *Rising* you've long known about Kamala's spectacular drop out of top-tier status into single digit obscurity. She's even had to watch as her tormenter Tulsi Gabbard, who she famously dissed as irrelevant and unworthy of a response, surpassed her in any number of polls. Well, the elite media has finally caught up with our analysis. Over the break both the *New York Times* and the *Washington Post* published well reported and devastatingly brutal pieces about exactly how Kamala's campaign came apart.

The New York Times
November 29, 2019
Headline: How Kamala Harris's Campaign Unraveled
Ms. Harris is the only 2020 Democrat who has fallen hard out of the top tier of candidates. She has proved to be an uneven campaigner who changes her message and tactics to little effect and has a staff torn into factions.
By Jonathan Martin, Astead W. Herndon, and Alexander Burns

The Times even went so far as to call into question whether Harris would ultimately make it to Iowa, writing:

> "After beginning her candidacy with a speech before 20,000 people in Oakland, some of Ms. Harris's longtime supporters believe she should consider dropping out in

216

late December — the deadline for taking her name off the California primary ballot — if she does not show political momentum."

So there you have it: Don't be surprised if Kamala is out of the race before the New Year. A stunning fall for a candidate who the media celebrated in the beginning, and who seemed to have a credible path to the nomination with California voting early.

By the way, when you start to see these pieces about inner campaign turmoil, it means that various internal campaign factions, advisors, and consultants are all trying to throw each other under the bus and pass the campaign's failure off on whoever they happen to hate the most. It's a surefire sign of a team that knows it will lose badly. The only thing left to fight for is the patina of dignity that comes from being able to claim that everything would have gone much better if only those in charge had listened to you.

Kamala's state director went so far as to quit altogether while releasing a blistering resignation letter in which she stated in part: "...because we have refused to confront our mistakes, foster an environment of critical thinking and honest feedback, or trust the expertise of talented staff, we find ourselves making the same unforced errors over and over."

What are those same unforced errors to which Kamala's Former State Director referred? Well, we can only guess at what they were referencing, but what we can say for certain is that you can't have a conference call to figure out what your core values are. If you don't know why you're running and what case you want to make to voters, if you don't actually know what you want to fight for, then no consultant or donor or advisor is going to be able to tell you. Instead you'll end up as Kamala did. Changing slogans with the seasons, moving in one aide's words from "'speak truth' spring" to "'3 a.m.' summer" to the current "'justice' winter." Voters will see through all of it: revealing someone who wants to be President for their own sake, not for the sake of the country.

Of course, Kamala's Medicare-for-All mess has been particularly instructive. You will recall that Kamala wrapped herself around Bernie's Medicare-for-All bill, going so far as to co-sponsor it in the Senate. Not only that, she built a portion of her initial presidential campaign list with Facebook ads expressing her pride in being the first Senator to support Bernie's Medicare-for-All bill. Then, she got some negative polling or consultant advice or donor pushback on this whole crazy notion of getting *everyone* healthcare. Soon enough, she was telling a room full of donors in the Hamptons that she had "not been comfortable with Bernie's plan," which she chucked in favor of whatever incomprehensible Medicare-for-the-Justice-Winter plan she's got now.

No surprise that while in June, a not too shabby 10 percent of voters said they trusted Kamala most on healthcare, now only three percent say the same. The leader on this metric is, of course, the guy who *"wrote the damn bill,"* followed closely by Joe Biden, who has been unwavering in his support of a more limited Affordable Care Act expansion. What's the lesson? Knowing what you stand for, articulating it clearly, and appearing ready to fight for it is more important than finding precisely the right poll-tested place to be on any particular issue. Voters may not be health care experts, but they can sure smell B.S. a mile away.

Kamala's downfall is also a warning to Elizabeth Warren, because she has also made major missteps on the issue that voters consistently tell pollsters is their number one concern. For Warren: first, she's with Bernie, then she says Medicare-for-All is a 'framework,' then she agonizes for weeks over how to avoid saying the words middle-class taxes, finally releasing a "transition plan" that exposed once and for all her fundamental unseriousness on the issue.

Unlike Kamala, Warren *does* actually have a core. At her core, she is a smart and serious technocrat with a passion for consumer protection and banking reform, but rather than embrace her core, she's faltered, trying to be all things to all people. She wants to be the revolutionary, talking about class warfare and a strain of militant unionism that she has frankly never been part of. But she also wants to be the girl-power feminist with her all-female campaign co-chairs and pink Planned Parenthood scarf, and by focusing only on the women who struggled in that labor movement that again she was never really part of. All the while, Warren also wants to be a team player who can position herself as exciting like Bernie, but without being scary. Let me just spoil the ending here and tell you that you can't be a revolutionary who is non-threatening to the establishment. In the end, you will just be unsatisfying to all.

If you want to know how quickly the wheels can come off, just ask Kamala Harris. After all, she may have some extra time coming up here in the New Year.

My Fight With A Billionaire And What It Reveals About The American Right

Saagar Enjeti

As someone on the right, it often irks me that so many on my side fail to call out those in power who are so obviously morally and financially corrupt. So many of our so-called leaders from Washington to Wall Street to Silicon Valley couldn't care less about the American people; their main concern is often their pocketbook, whether or not that pocketbook is directly tied to authoritarian governments like China. And yet, while selling a lie about 'fiscal responsibility' to a working-class America that works paycheck-to-paycheck—mothers and fathers who probably know much more about being financially responsible and stretching a dollar than those who sit and scoff from their ivory towers—they use power and influence to maneuver the system to benefit them and their interests, often on the backs of the people that they purportedly represent.

I see a vision for a new kind of conservatism: one that puts working families and communities first, ahead of the interests of elite, coastal cities. I see a future that actually respects and champions hard work—one that makes sure families can raise children under one roof with a single income if they choose, with healthcare, and without fear that their jobs will be automated away or shipped overseas as a result of disastrous trade deals. I see a future that values stable, meaningful livelihoods over 'cheap' imported products for a massive consumer base. I see a future that values sovereignty and American values over world-policing and the interests of a few liberal Ivy League graduates at the top.

Much of what I have talked about on the show, and that has frankly resonated with so many from the left to the right, is the need for Republicans to distance themselves from libertarianism. Sure, I believe restraint abroad is fundamental and important; but, no, I don't think that we should back down from a rising China that threatens our way of life, both socially and economically. No, I am not a socialist, but I do believe that our government has a moral responsibility to protect the important institutions that built this country: workers and families. That may take the form of national industrial policy that harnesses the power of American industry, as we did in World War II, while protecting the communities that families across the country grew up in and love. I also believe that while the donors and backroom dealers may not like it, we should have serious conversations about health care and ensure paid family leave. I also don't believe that a few morally shameful and crooked Silicon Valley tech bros should be able to hold so much power over the rest of us, including what we think, and how we speak. None of that is libertarian—but it is right. Not only is it right, but it is the future.

Some of the most recent political studies done in the post-Trump era show that many are not as "socially liberal, fiscally conservative," or *libertarian*, when thinking about national policy. Yet, libertarians—those with the same kind of thought process as the millionaires and billionaires that often dominate the national conversation, have a stranglehold on D.C. institutions and financial industries. A recent incident, wherein I got into a bit of a Twitter spat with a hedge fund manager, highlighted the problem with libertarians in a way that I will never forget. Enjoy this monologue about that in the following pages.

December 30, 2019

Over a nice holiday break, I was minding my own business, rubbing the sleep from my eyes in the Rocky Mountains, when an interesting thing happened. I checked my phone to see billionaire hedge fund manager Clifford Asness rage tweeting about a monologue that I did on *Rising* about how the Right must ditch libertarianism. Clifford, a hedge fund manager worth about 2.6 billion dollars, and an avowed libertarian, had this to say about my take: "There is nothing libertarian about crony capitalism, libertarians have called it out first and loudest. But mediocre (I'm being nice) nobody braying populists of the right now think they're edgy and sound smart by decrying them, spitting out the word 'libertarian' like a curse." He followed up by explaining why he felt the need to block me: "Yes, I tweeted that, then blocked him, as I'm not getting into a back and forth with this fool. I just won't be able to be my normal gentlemanly self. Weak? Yes. Necessary? I think so."

Let's leave aside the fact that a man worth 2.6 billion dollars behaves like a kindergarten child online, and get to the substance of his argument.

Clifford Asness is an avowed libertarian against crony capitalism, he says. And yet, it turns out that in November 2016, he accepted 35 million dollars in tax breaks from the state of Connecticut in order to keep his business there. Sounds a lot like crony capitalism, huh? I responded, with an attached headline about his big payoff:

> @esaagar: "Billionaire @cliffordasness is apparently very triggered by one of my past monologues denouncing libertarians. So much so he tweeted this and then blocked me. If one of you could remind him of this one his timeline it would be great."

When confronted by so many of you who answered my call to action to confront him with this obvious hypocrisy, this is what Clifford had to say:

> @CliffordAsness: "When the government as a whole takes half your income and part of it offers to give a small amount back over many years, not as a handout but contingent on creating more jobs, it's a small rebate anyone would take. But you won't see this as you're blocked.

> @CliffordAsness: Yes I expected this. A) nobody hacks get very excited when they're blocked by someone who's just a bit more than a nobody, exciting day for him B)

silly NYT agitprop from a "conservative"; Paul Krugman has also attacked me multiple times. He didn't look hard enough for allies.

Clifford essentially believes that since he's paid taxes over the years, in exchange for "creating jobs," that he is entitled to his little tax break from the state of Connecticut. In other words, Clifford is A-OK with the government giving tax breaks to businesses as long as they create jobs — old Clifford is a proponent of an industrial policy for the business that he himself happens to have a hand in, and not for others.

I've invited Clifford to come on this show and debate me, as all principled libertarians on YouTube love to do, but I won't hold my breath. Clifford's bizarre online meltdown ultimately culminated in his admitting that he didn't handle himself very well, but it was far more revealing for the way corporatists in the Republican and Democratic parties operate. They denounce government intervention in markets unless that government intervention is helpful to the sectors that they operate in, like, say, hedge funds.

The New York Times
November 22, 2016
Headline: Investment Funds Get Millions to Stay in Connecticut

Cliff Asness, co-founder of AQR Capital Management. His firm is set to receive $35 million in incentives from the state of Connecticut
By Alexandra Stevenson

Interestingly enough, at the time that Clifford got himself a nice tax rebate, the state comptroller denounced the handout as "financial welfare," given that a tax break could instead have been given to manufacturing businesses to create stable middle-class jobs, rather than financial firms who only employ graduates from top-tier universities, who would have no problem getting a job in any state.

Clifford's libertarian braying online, coupled with his obvious hypocrisy, tells you the story of the American financial elite over the last many decades. They claim to operate in the free market, and then they take bailouts, handouts, tax breaks, and any other corporate welfare that they can get their grubby hands on, while lobbying tooth-and-nail to ensure that productive enterprises, which actually employ working-class people, have no access to the same resources.

Clifford Asness's corrupt and indignant hypocrisy is exactly the corporatism that I was calling out in the monologue that so deeply offended him. Libertarianism, in practice, is a selective corporate welfare ideology pushed by the financial industry and big business in Washington to justify the myriad of government subsidies and benefits that prop up the very foundations of their businesses. All the new right is asking for is that maybe all that government attention should be given to the working class of this country instead.

Against Crenshaw Conservatism

Saagar Enjeti

One of the things that animates me most on *Rising* is tracking and participating in the fight for the future of the GOP after Trump. Donald Trump demonstrated in 2016 that breaking from free-market orthodoxy while defending family values can yield massive electoral dividends.

The only problem is that Trump's departure from free-market orthodoxy alienates the very party bosses and donors who have controlled the party for nearly 40 years. The Paul Ryans of the world, the Koch brothers, and innumerable numbers of Wall Street billionaires have undergone a multi-decade effort to make free-market libertarian ideals the unwavering economic position of the GOP.

These people did not simply roll over and die when Donald Trump was elected. Instead what they did was don red Make America Great Again hats while spouting the same B.S. ideology that they always have. Trump, not knowing any better, takes them as his genuine supporters — when in reality they are snakes ready to take the party right back to 2012 after he is gone.

No person better exemplifies this trend than GOP star Congressman Dan Crenshaw. Crenshaw is a decorated Navy SEAL, who no doubt has shown grace in the public eye during his spat with SNL star Pete Davidson. The problem, however, is that

Crenshaw is a through and through economic libertarian in his speech.

This essay was written after Crenshaw told his Twitter followers that Uber was what conservatism really should be, reviving an oft-repeated talking point of economic libertarians within the Republican Party from back in 2012. It is my attempt at dismantling this disaster of an ideology and charting a new working-class friendly path forward for the GOP.

November 18, 2019

As I've said here on the show many times before, my greatest fear for the GOP after Trump is a bunch of people chanting 'Drain the Swamp!' with MAGA hats on while actually pushing zombie Reagan ideology with a Trumpian flair.

That fear was realized earlier this weekend when GOP rising star Congressman Dan Crenshaw Tweeted, "In 2020, remember this: Republicans are the party of Uber. Democrats are the party of taxi cab unions. Own your own labor, work where you want and how you want, and embrace innovation. That's conservatism." I was stunned to be reading those words in the year 2019, from someone who purports to represent the Trump agenda. Did I die and wake up in 2014? Is Paul Ryan still Speaker; are we doing makers-versus-takers again?

Look, I hold Crenshaw in high esteem. His service to our country is unquestioned, he showed class and grace at the height of his fame after the SNL incident, and on matters such as illegal immigration, he has been a stalwart. But it's the economy, stupid!

'Crenshaw Conservatism' will doom the GOP to major losses in future elections, and more importantly, it betrays the very reason why so many untold millions were willing to give Donald Trump a chance at the Oval Office in the first place. Let's ignore the fact that Crenshaw is holding up a company that loses billions of dollars a year as the face of American conservatism, and go a little bit deeper.

Manhattan Institute Senior Fellow Oren Cass pointed out after Crenshaw's Tweet that "calling your opponents 'the party of Uber'" is a "truly low blow," given that it "provides unstable, poorly paid, part-time work that is not a stepping stone to anything and almost never can support a family." Crenshaw was quickly piled on, so he added this addendum via Tweet:

> "1. Working for a company is a CHOICE. Terms of that relationship are made clear from the start. 2. The gig economy provides flexibility that we otherwise wouldn't have. If you prevent companies from using independent contractors, you're ENDING millions of jobs."

Again, Crenshaw misses the mark. Yes, Uber represents a major technological innovation, but from an economic perspective, it basically represents eliminating the obligations of employer-employee relations and makes any sort of competition with an entity that needs to balance its books impossible, not to mention the epidemic of rising suicides amongst their workforce and in the country as a whole.

As Cass again masterfully points out, Uber's entire case is that the drivers don't actually work for them! Saying that is only slightly less embarrassing for the Congressman than the effort to revive a position discredited 100 years ago—that individual low-wage workers have the market power to dictate terms and conditions of employment.

We understood 100 years ago that corporate power has as much, if not more, control over the everyday lives of American citizens than the government. That's why we stepped in to provide protections codified in law and we took actions to preserve competition in our marketplace.

Fetishizing gig work, fake job creation, and expanding GDP numbers ignores the very things that make life worth living. As author Chris Arnade excellently said on Twitter this weekend, "I still can't believe there's anyone alive who doesn't understand that focusing only on things that 'can be measured' while ignoring & destroying than those that can't, like the value of faith, place, family, and community, is our problem."

For many years, 'Crenshaw Conservatives' told us that neoliberal free trade policy, corporate tax cuts, bank bailouts, and celebrating companies like Uber were how you both preserve, protect, and expand the everyday quality of life for Americans. We know how it all worked out—the hollowing out of the American middle class, skyrocketing costs for needs of American life, crippling debt, declining birth rates, declining life expectancy, a historic opioid epidemic, and record-high suicide rates.

The GOP's singular focus should be to orient all domestic and foreign policy towards a single goal: easing the ability to make enough money and have reasonable enough costs to start a bountiful family in the place of your choosing. If they forget that, they'll never win back power, no matter how many corporate checks they cash.

The Populist's Guide to Governing

Krystal Ball

"A Pipe Dream." That's what mercenary corporate tool and former Obama Chief of Staff Rahm Emanuel called Medicare-for-All. He's not the first or the last to dismiss Bernie Sanders and his ideas as impractical or insane or radical or fanciful. These same voices of "reason" also love to argue for their own absurdly delusional fantasy in which Republicans post-Trump will suddenly open their hearts in good faith to Democrats for the good of the country.

I have to admit, of course, none of the significant changes Sanders is calling for will be easily won. The Green New Deal, Medicare-for-All, College-for-All, Broadband-for-All. It's an ambitious agenda, and any President would be lucky to get a fraction of it accomplished. But when Bernie gets asked about how he will accomplish it, he has a consistent answer: such big changes will require a political revolution. It's easy to think of this "political revolution" in vague and squishy terms, but Sanders actually means something very specific when he says it. He plans more or less to run the same playbook nationally that he used to create a true political revolution in formerly conservative Burlington, Vermont.

I had a kind of "a ha" moment when I listened to a New York Times interview with Sanders for their podcast The Daily, in which they dug deep into his time as Mayor. For me it helped elucidate exactly how far the establishment of both parties would likely go to stop a President Sanders from finding success. It also made me realize that he knows exactly how hard they will fight him and has a plan for how to win.

December 10, 2019

One of the central ideas we hit often on this show is Theory of Change. Outside versus inside. Grassroots versus top-down. Negotiation versus revolution.

The New York Times
November 27, 2019
Headline: Bernie Sanders vs. The Machine

In 1981, he was elected mayor of Burlington. But the city's bureacracy showed him that winning wasn't everything. So he learned to fight back.
By Alexander Burns

Bernie Sanders just gave a lengthy and fascinating interview to Michael Barbaro over at *The New York Times'* podcast *The Daily*, written up for print by Alex Burns. They decided to focus on Bernie's stunning 10-vote-victory to become mayor of Burlington, Vermont in 1981. Up to that point, Sanders had run a series of protest campaigns, always garnering just a few points. But he caught the entitled incumbent sleeping, built an unprecedented coalition of working-class people, and eked out a stunning victory. Just imagine the shock of the nation to see a socialist mayor coming to power at the height of the Cold War. His victory garnered national coverage and was even featured in an amazing segment on the Today Show:

> *Jane Pauley: "Face it, you don't find too many socialists in elected office in this country, and when one is elected mayor of a sizeable city, well that's news. It's also Phil Donahue's topic this morning."*
>
> *Phil Donahue: "Good morning, Jane. A couple of facts. Burlington is the largest city in Vermont. The state has about half a million people. Burlington has about 38,000. Situated as it is on Lake Champlain with the Adirondack mountains viewable, it is a lovely, lovely spot in this country. We'd like you to meet its*

new mayor. This is mayor Bernard Sanders. Mayor Sanders got a lot of attention recently, not only with his ten vote victory, out of about 9,500 votes cast, but mostly because he is a socialist. And everybody reading that article said 'My goodness, how did this happen in good old conservative Vermont?'"

The story of the campaign itself is interesting. Burlington was essentially a one-party town. The Democrats had such a lock on city hall, and there was so little difference between them and the GOP, that the Republicans weren't even fielding a candidate. But Sanders noticed that in his previous quixotic statewide races he had actually over-performed in the working-class neighborhoods of Burlington, an early indication that fed-up working-class citizens were desperate for a non-mainstream alternative. So he decided to run, figuring out electoral politics on the fly, stunning the political establishment and the entire nation.

What really fascinated me, though, was what happened after Sanders was elected. There he was after this amazing upset: Mayor of Burlington. And all of the powers that be, whether Republican or Democrat, decided that Sanders was a fluke. In words frequently applied these days to Donald Trump, he was seen as an *aberration*. An abnormality. A one-and-done. So the Board of Aldermen, essentially their City Council, devised a strategy. They would obstruct everything Sanders tried to do. Prove to the city that he was incompetent at governing and get back to their bipartisan status quo consensus.

The Board of Alderman started by blocking all of Sanders' key appointments—even his secretary. Mayor Sanders was forced to try to run the city with all of his predecessor's obstructionists still in place. In the interview, Sanders compared this situation to Trump having to run the government with all of Obama's cabinet members in place, which of course is more-or-less what Trump thinks has happened to him. But while Trump has collapsed into an endless stream of conspiracy-mongering and Twitter grievances, Sanders figured out how to get around the obstruction and govern the city according to his values.

Sanders got together some of his top supporters and formed a shadow government to help craft and execute ideas. He also relied directly on the people of the city, delegating power to neighborhood councils. Each borough was given its own budget that it could allocate independently to suit the needs of the community.

One year into Mayor Sanders' term, seven of the 13 establishment aldermen were up for reelection in what Sanders describes as essentially a referendum on his administration. This was truly a do or die moment for him. Would his political revolution be upheld or rejected in Burlington? Sanders fielded his own slate of five candidates. He tells *The New York Times* that he worked harder than he's ever worked in his life, knocking on almost every door of the city with the candidates by his side. When all the votes were counted, three of Sanders' candidates won outright and two forced the incumbents into runoffs. The remaining establishment Democrats were actually forced to team up with the Republicans to keep control of the board, the Burlington equivalent of Chuck Schumer voting for Mitch McConnell for majority leader!

But perhaps most significantly, in one year's time, Sanders doubled voter turnout, dramatically increasing the level of popular participation, and bringing the citizens back into engagement with their city government. Sanders could no longer be written off as a fluke, but rather a force in his own right with a base of power independent from any political party. He then went on to win reelection three times, including once against a candidate who was backed by both major parties. Because the one thing that brings establishment Democrats and Republicans together is their commitment to defeating anyone with their own working-class base of support.

In his interview with *the New York Times*, Bernie explained his electoral success in Burlington this way: "What that tells me is that if the government does respond to the needs of working people, they will come out and participate." A simple statement, but one at such odds with the suppression, manipulation, caricature, and derision that working people are typically subjected to.

To me, this interview was so revealing because you can see all of the parallels with his political philosophy and theory of change today. He has faith in this idea of a political revolution because he's done it and seen it. Remember this moment recently when John Harwood, Editor-at-Large for CNBC, asked how he would handle someone like Joe Manchin opposing Medicare-for-All?

> *John Harwood: "Is Joe Manchin going to vote for your program, is Jon Tester going to vote for your program?"*
>
> *Bernie Sanders: "Damn right they will. You know why? And they're friends of mine. We're going to go to West Virginia which is maybe the poorest state — one of the poorest states in this country — look what happens right now is your average politician sits around and he or she thinks, 'If I do this, I'm going to have the big money interest putting 30 second ads against me, so I better not do it. But now they're going to have to think, if I don't support an agenda that works for working people, I'm going to have President Sanders come into my state and rally working-class people. You know what, at the end of the day, the one percent is very powerful. No denying that. The 99 percent when they're organized and prepared to stand up and fight, they are far more powerful."*

Just as he did in Burlington, Sanders is putting his faith not in some mythical negotiating power as Trump did, or in some fantasy of coming to the table in good faith negotiations with Mitch McConnell as Biden and Obama and Buttigieg do, or even in his ability to jiujitsu the levers of government through superior bureaucratic knowledge as Warren does. He believes, just as he did in Burlington, that the only way to break the back of Congressional gridlock and inertia and neoliberal entrenchment is by putting your faith in people. In serving as the Organizer-in-Chief.

Obviously the federal government is a different deal than Burlington, Vermont. There are way more corrupt lawmakers, lobbyists, and donors sucking at the government teat. There is an entire national media arrayed against you just looking for damaging leaks and to spin stories to destroy you in every way possible. But you've also got a lot more citizens available to have your back and new modes of communicating to circumvent the elite media, something Sanders has very deliberately cultivated.

Just as he doubled voter participation in Burlington,

breaking the back of the establishment lock on city politics, if McConnell and Manchin and Pelosi, et al. stand in his way and block passage of popular legislation to benefit the working-class citizens, he is counting on a reckoning—a massive show of electoral force that would bring a tidal wave of new voters into the system, creating a new accountability for those who would stand in their way. That's what political revolution looked like in Burlington, and that's what he believes it will look like in D.C.

Afterword

This book is a reflection of and a response to the current political realignment happening before our eyes. It is a curated daily snapshot into that realignment as we tried to understand and explain the day-to-day politics of the last year and it underscores, above all, that the old ways of looking at politics as conventionally liberal and conservative are no longer useful.

Elections are in many ways like a natural experiment through which people in Washington get to find out what actual Americans think about their job performance. Their sheer inability to predict the rise and resilience of Donald Trump revealed just how little they know about the country they govern. Their consistent ignoring of the Bernie Sanders, Andrew Yang, and Tulsi Gabbard phenomena today tells you that they have learned nothing.

This book comes at a critical time of working-class uprisings across the globe, from Donald Trump's election, the rise of Bernie Sanders' political movement, the overwhelming support for Brexit in the British election, to a myriad of protests on nearly every continent. And yet, you turn on your TV just to find talking heads and so-called analysts talking about whatever uncouth thing that Donald Trump Tweeted a few minutes ago. If they deign to cover global uprising, they will shove numbers in your face or repeat antiquated theories about how the global population has never been better off because a World Bank index says so.

The media, the professional class, and the establishment of both parties refuse to grapple with the reality that Americans face. They do not know what it is like to work incredibly hard all day and then attend a class they can barely afford at night, wondering if they will have to choose between rent or a meal. They know nothing of what it's like struggling to find daycare for your kids because you or your partner can't stay home to raise your children, or forgo a doctor's appointment and grit your teeth in pain because you simply don't have the funds. We cannot live in a society where a huge segment of the population is a blown tire away from bankruptcy.

We've attempted to outline for you how the American economy is fundamentally not structured for the success of its working class, how the mass media acts more as a propaganda tool of the powerful rather than as a societal check, how identity politics is cynically used by elites to keep workers from claiming their destiny, and offered you two important visions for how to build a more equitable future for this country.

These aren't partisan beliefs; they're a set of truths about our democracy, so you can understand the choices we have and paths we face. The reality for the working class is not an accident, it's a deliberate design by the professional-managerial class in Washington who want workers to serve as cogs in an engineered system that places no value on family or community.

The problem at the core of our society is not necessarily "left" or "right," it's that the center shared by those in the Republican and Democratic parties is rotten to its core, and abetted by the most powerful people in the United States.

The good news is that we live in a representative democracy, unlike so many of those who are participating in global uprising movements around the world. The lesson of 2016 and beyond is that people are hungry for a politics that exists to serve them—the people. Not a politics that serves the most wealthy, or the luckiest college grads with a new job at McKinsey & Co., or that tells coal miners to "learn to code" and champions the interests of a few billionaires at the top, or a foreign country ready to offer a "better deal."

A *Jacobin* profile of our show recently wrote that watching it is like "you just woke up a decade into some mass political realignment, in which the Bloombergians, the Paul Ryans, the Clintonites, and even the Obamicans have all been swept into the dustbin of history, leaving only two poles standing: Bernie Sanders and Steve Bannon."

That is our vision for the future. Two parties united in the belief that the working class of this country has been screwed for too long and squabbling instead over how to improve their lot in life. If there is a bipartisan consensus in Washington, let it not be on war, let it not be predicated on the idea that financial markets are better off when they're unregulated—let it instead be that the current state of our society is unacceptable.

Krystal is fighting for a Democratic Party that reclaims its roots as the party of the people. A party that would discard the extreme capitalist thinking which says that you are only worthy of dignity if you live in a certain zip code, were born into privilege, or happen to have a brain that excels in ways valued by "the market." In a wealthy country, the good life shouldn't be for a lucky few. The current massive inequality, depression, and loss of meaning isn't sustainable or good for anyone. She wants a Democratic Party that rips power from the hands of the elites and distributes it to the working class men and women who bleed and die in unjust wars, and have been shut out of the economic fruits of their own labor.

Saagar demands a new kind of conservatism: one that puts working families and communities first, ahead of the interests of elite, coastal cities. A future that actually respects and champions hard work—one that makes sure families can raise children under one roof with a single income if they choose, with healthcare, and without fear that their jobs will be automated away or shipped overseas as a result of disastrous trade deals. A future that values stable, meaningful livelihoods over 'cheap' imported products for a massive consumer base and a future that values sovereignty and American values over world-policing and the interests of a few liberal Ivy League graduates at the top. This conservatism would have the single, fundamental, uniting goal that every American deserves prosperity in a place of their choosing.

At the end of the day, the ideas that animate us are quite simple, and center around a singular idea. The American families, workers, and communities which built this country still matter, they deserve a voice, and they are the future.

Acknowledgments

It has been wild to watch the response to Rising over the past year and so we have to start by thanking everyone involved in making it a success every day! First of all, thank you to Jimmy Finkelstein for taking a chance on us and on a new vision for a morning show. We are forever grateful for his willingness to embrace a new approach to news and politics. Thank you to Ryan Grim for giving us the best insights and believing in the vision for this book! Thank you to superstar Jake Mercier for giving up his Christmas break to edit and assemble this book, you are the greatest and we are routinely stunned by your intellect, idealism, and passion.

Our show of course would not be possible without the talented and amazing staff we have at Rising who wake up early every morning to make sure we are able to bring it in the way the audience expects. Special thanks to Rhonda who not only makes us look our best but brings energy, spunk, and style to what we do every day. And to Buck Sexton for launching this show initially alongside Krystal. He helped set the course for a new type of political conversation and the show today would not be possible without his early work.

Thank you so much to our fellow alt-media brothers and sisters! Jimmy Dore, Kyle Kulinski, Michael Brooks, Tim Black, Cenk, Ana, Emma and the whole Young Turks crew. You all have been such a source of inspiration, solidarity, business sense and friendship. We are incredibly grateful.

We're also grateful to all of the Rising guests who inform, challenge and shape our views every day. An inestimable number of the ideas in this book were sparked and polished by the guests who give us their time every morning. Thank you to you all!

But most of all, thank you to the millions of people who tune in to Rising for something different and whose energy and attention give voice to the multi-racial working class. You are the reason we get up every morning and you are the ones who are going to work to make this country what it should and could be.

Krystal: I want to thank my first mentor in television and the first person to put me on air, the first person to advocate at MSNBC for me to have a show, the original visionary behind the modern Today show and a TV legend, the inimitable Steve Friedman. I adore you Steve and I think about your lessons in this the medium every day.

Whatever success I have, both my grounding in trying to be a decent human being and my attempting to be courageous in the world, I owe to my parents, Dr. Edwin Ball and Rose Marie Ball. Thank you to my Dad for being an independent thinker with an insatiable intellectual curiosity. Thank you to my Mom for being an absolute unyielding force of nature whose courage and compassion are limitless. Thanks to both for your absolutely unconditional no strings attached love.

To my husband Jonathan, my greatest ambition is to live up to your image of me! Thank you for your brilliance, unshakeable faith, and for always keeping me off balance. There is no way I would have had the confidence to be outspoken or take the risks that I've taken without your encouragement and support and knowledge that no matter how badly I screwed up, you would still choose me over every other woman on the planet. I love you!

Thank you to my crazy, curious, hilarious, brilliant kiddos. Ella the curious. Lowell the wild. Ida Rose the force. You guys are the greatest and I love you more than anything!

Saagar: I would like to thank my parents Radhika Viruru

and Prasad Enjeti who encouraged and supported my, at times, annoying obsession with politics from a very young age. I'd be remiss if I didn't also thank my sister Sahiti Enjeti who was a bystander to my rants and musings in many long drives. This book would not be possible without the support of my best friend Marshall Kosloff, my girlfriend Jillian McGrath, the c21 organization, the Hudson Institute and so many more in Washington DC who have supported my work. I especially want to thank all of those at The Daily Caller who gave my first shot at a job in media from Neil Patel, Tucker Carlson, Geoffrey Ingersoll, Vince Coglianese, Christopher Bedford, and so many of my original colleagues at The DCNF. I remember most all those who responded to my emails when I was a 22 year old asking to grab coffee or talk on the phone and took time out of their busy day to help me, thank you all - I will never forget it.

CPSIA information can be obtained
at www.ICGtesting.com
Printed in the USA
LVHW050030040220
645691LV00005B/878